Country Living

Cookies & Crackers

· COUNTRY BAKER ·

Cookies & Crackers

THE EDITORS OF
COUNTRY LIVING MAGAZINE

Foreword by Rachel Newman

Country Living

HEARST BOOKS · NEW YORK

Copyright © 1993 by THE HEARST CORPORATION

Photography Credits
Pages 17, 72, Richard Jeffery
Pages 18, 35, 36, 54, 71, Jerry Simpson
Page 53, Charles Gold

•

•

It is the policy of William Morrow and Company, Inc., and its imprints and affiliates,
recognizing the importance of preserving what has been written, to print the books we
publish on acid-free paper, and we exert our best efforts to that end.

•

Library of Congress Cataloging-in-Publication Data
Country Living.
Country living, country baker. Cookies & crackers :
foreword by Rachel Newman. — 1st ed.
p. cm.
Includes index.
ISBN 0-688-12542-5 (alk. paper)
1. Cookies. 2. Crackers. I. Country living (New York, N.Y.)
II. Title. III. Title: Country baker. IV. Title: Cookies & crackers.
V. Title: Cookies and crackers.
TX772.C663   1993
641.8'654—dc20   92-33223
                                                  CIP

•

Printed in Singapore
First Edition
2 3 4 5 6 7 8 9 10

•

Country Living Staff
Rachel Newman, Editor-in-Chief
Lucy Wing, Contributing Food Editor
Joanne Lamb Hayes, Food Editor
Elaine Van Dyne, Associate Food Editor

Produced by Smallwood and Stewart, Inc., New York City

Edited by Judith Blahnik
Designed by Tom Starace
Cover designed by Lynn Pieroni Fowler

Contents

AMERICAN COOKIE CLASSICS...................................11

From old New England hermits and thumbprints to snickerdoodles, these are cookies that quickly disappear from dessert platters all over America.

Hermits, Linzer Hearts, Benne Seed Wafers, Coconut Macaroons, Almond Oaties, Apricot-Oat Thumbprints, Gingham Cookies, Cornmeal Cookies, Snickerdoodles, Spongeware Cookies, Gingersnaps, Spritz Cookies

TEA COOKIES 27

Here is our assortment of buttery sweet cookies. All of them are easy to make and all are elegant enough for a fancy tea tray. And shortbread lovers celebrate! There are three butter-rich renditions here.

Chocolate Cookie Hearts, Delectabites, Orange Raisin Shortbread, Chocolate Wafers, Raisin-Pecan Crescents, Shortbread, Hazelnut Shortbread, Pistachio Biscotti

BARS & BROWNIES 37

Our collection of brownies and bar cookies proves how versatile these simple cookies are. We share with you our favorites — from dense brownie chocolate bars to creamy squares redolent of lemon.

Brownies, Blondies, Rhubarb Oatmeal Bars, Caramel-Pistachio Brownies, Peanut Butter Brownies, Prune-Nut Bars, Coffee Snack Bars, Fig Bars, Fruitcake Patchwork Squares, Oatmeal Cranberry Bars, Rhubarb Raisin Squares, Lemon Squares, Fruit Bars

COOKIE JAR FAVORITES 55
The fantasy of anyone who reaches into the cookie jar is to pull out one of these giant versions of America's most popular cookies.

Spiral Cookies, Peanut Butter Cookies, Zebra Cookies, Chocolate-Chip Cookies, Oatmeal Raisin Cookies, Peanut Butter and Jelly Cookies, Chocolate Chocolate-Chip Cookies, Black and Whites

NEIGHBORHOOD SPECIALTIES 64
Here are the special-occasion cookies such as marshmallow puffs and triple chocolate chips that were famous, if not in your house, then in your neighborhood. Dozens of them show up at potlucks and bake sales.

Almond Cookies, Mocha Macadamia Cookies, Swirled Lemon Cookies, Chocolate Chunk Cookies, Sugar-Cookie Butterflies, Sesame Cookies, Prune-Pumpkin Cookies, Raisin Filled Cookies, Pistachio-Mint Chocolate Cookies, Triple Chocolate-Chip Cookies, Marshmallow Puffs

COUNTRY CRACKERS & CRISPS............................80
Since the mid-1800s, when commercially made crackers first appeared, the output of home-baked crackers has plummeted. To remedy this, we've collected some old cracker recipes that are authentic, delicious, and remarkably easy to make.

Cheddar Crackers, Johnnycake Crisps, Old-Fashioned Soda Crackers, Whole-Wheat Crackers, Cracker Wheels, Cornmeal Crisps

Foreword

....

A fter many years of working on women's magazines, I learned that there are certain recipes readers ask for over and over again. None can compare with their interest in cookie recipes, especially at holiday time. The tradition of baking cookies for family gatherings, for gifts, and for entertaining dates back generations. Amazingly, it seems that no matter how many recipes we have in our *Country Living* files, there is always room — and demand — for more.

Today there is also more interest than ever in recipes for homemade crackers and fruit bars. In these health-conscious times people are especially watchful and cautious about buying packaged food that might contain chemical additives, artificial flavors, and harmful preservatives. It is truly satisfying to know that only the purest ingredients are going into the food that you're serving your family and friends.

While some people treat cookie recipes as treasured family secrets, we're bringing ours into the open, to be shared and enjoyed. But be careful — as soon as word gets out about the treats coming from your oven, you might not be able to keep up with the requests for more.

Rachel Newman
Editor-in-Chief

Introduction

WHENEVER COOKIES BURN IN THE KITCHEN, AN UNHAPPY
CHILD MAKES A PLAN TO RUN AWAY FROM HOME.

J. M. Barrie

As Americans, we make cookies for nearly every important celebration. Platters mounded with decorated cookies appear at holidays, weddings, birthdays, celebrations of births, and even wakes. We make them part of our everyday lives, too, thinking nothing of turning out a quick batch of walnut refrigerator cookies for a school lunch box, or presenting a plate of date-nut bars to a new neighbor, or simply taking pleasure in filling the cookie jar with the old-fashioned oatmeal-raisin, peanut butter, and chocolate chip cookies of our own childhoods.

We are less afraid of making cookies than of doing any other food chore in the kitchen. It's as if Americans were born with a cookie gene, and turning out a batch seems to come naturally. It's a rite of passage for the young ones in the house — the kitchen event that proves to the child that she or he is creative and capable and can bring about sweet miracles from simple mounds of dough.

Our *Country Living* collection is a tribute to the diversity of cookies that thrives in our American culture. Here are more than fifty recipes for the buttery, crispy, moist and soft, small and dainty, gigantic, plain, frosted, simple, or packed with nuts cookies, bars, brownies, and shortbreads. Most of our recipes are quick and easy, while others are a bit more complicated. None are difficult.

About The Ingredients

Our recipes require unsifted all-purpose or whole-wheat flours unless otherwise noted. Other grains include oats, which might be the old-fashioned or quick-cooking rolled oats. Never use instant-cooking oats.

We use fresh double-acting baking powder. Check the date on the can to make sure yours is fresh. If there's any doubt, stir 1 teaspoonful into ½ cup hot water. If there's a bubbling reaction, the baking powder is fresh.

Butter is lightly salted and always in the stick, as is margarine, if you choose to use it. Don't substitute tub or whipped butter, or liquid or tub spread margarine. They contain more water and less fat than stick, and, while they may be better for you on the dinner table, they are not better for your baking.

The cocoa powder we use is unsweetened, and when we call for chocolate squares, they are the 1-ounce squares found in bakers' chocolate. Eggs are always large and stored, refrigerated, in their cartons. They are an important ingredient because of their binding effect. Do not use egg substitutes unless noted in the recipe.

We recommend using real not imitation vanilla, maple, and almond extracts. The pungent flavor of the authentic extract permeates and perfumes your cookies as no imitation can. Spices such as cinnamon, allspice, ginger, and cloves should be checked for freshness. If your jar or can is more than six months old, the spice may deliver disappointing results. Nutmeg is always best when grated from the whole nutmeg. When we call for walnuts, almonds, pecans, and hazelnuts, it's in their natural, unblanched state unless otherwise noted.

About The Equipment

Give yourself enough space and time to assemble ingredients before you begin to mix. Cookies turn out best when the ingredients are combined with dispatch and the batter is not overworked. Two different-size mixing bowls and a set of metal measuring cups for dry ingredients and glass measuring cups for liquids are essential for stress-free baking.

Bake the cookies in the size and type of pan or on the standard baking sheet we suggest. Baking sheets and pans of medium-weight restaurant-quality aluminum are the all-round best for optimum conduction of heat and even baking. Nonstick metal pans are good if you buy bonded rather than the sprayed-surface pans and grease them (just to guarantee their promises). Before buying a larger than standard baking

sheet, measure the inside of your oven to make sure the larger pan fits. The best sheets for baking cookies have low outer rims. This helps the heat circulate around the cookies as they bake.

12- by 15-inch baking sheet
14- by 17-inch baking sheet
8- and 9-inch square pans
13- by 9-inch rectangular pan
10-inch round cake pans at least 1½-inches deep
15½ -inch by 10½ inch jelly-roll pan
1¾-inch muffin-pan cups

Cookie cutters made of metal or plastic are invaluable and enhance the cookie making process tremendously. Keep an assortment of stars, trees, and animal shapes — and get some wreaths and angels for the holidays. Very thin cutters with sharp rims are ideal. Iron or clay cookie molds are expensive but can create exciting detail in the cookie. A pastry brush is handy for applying glazes. A rolling pin, cookie press with assorted attachments, and a pastry bag with assorted tips for decorating are also necessary.

A wire or wooden cooling rack is a must. The cookies must cool evenly on a surface that allows air to circulate. This will prevent the cookies from continuing to cook while they sit on the hot baking sheet.

About The Method

For the purposes of saving space, we have not described certain techniques in detail. When the recipe says cool completely on a wire rack, it means to cool the cookies to room temperature. When the recipe directs you to "remove the cookies from the pan," it means to loosen the cookies with a metal spatula and lift and place them on the cooling rack.

When the recipe says "cut out the cookie shapes and place on the baking sheet," it means to take a spatula to lift the cut cookie dough to gently place it on the baking sheet.

Hermits

....

Sailors from New England, setting out on clipper ships, would stow these in chests for long voyages. There are many variations, but the hearty hermit always includes lots of raisins, nuts, and spices.

MAKES ABOUT 6½ DOZEN COOKIES

1 cup (2 sticks) butter or margarine, softened
1½ cups firmly packed light-brown sugar
2 eggs
½ cup cold coffee
3½ cups all-purpose flour
1½ teaspoons ground cinnamon
1 teaspoon baking soda
½ teaspoon salt
½ teaspoon ground nutmeg
2 cups dark seedless raisins
1½ cups chopped walnuts or pecans

1. Heat the oven to 400°F. Grease 2 baking sheets. In a large bowl, with an electric mixer on medium speed, beat the butter and sugar until light and fluffy. Add the eggs and coffee; beat until blended. Reduce the mixer speed to low and beat in 1 cup flour, the cinnamon, baking soda, salt, and nutmeg just until combined. Stir in the remaining 2½ cups flour to form a stiff dough.

2. Stir the raisins and walnuts into the dough. Drop the dough by teaspoonfuls, about 2 inches apart, on the prepared baking sheets.

3. Bake the cookies 10 to 12 minutes, or until firm and lightly browned. Cool the cookies completely on wire racks.

A SMILE IN A NAME

New Englanders had a penchant for naming cookies so that they would be fun to talk about. Hermits and Snickerdoodles are good examples. Early Americans were responsible for other additions to the 18th Century cookie lexicon such as Graham Jakes, Jolly Boys, Brambles, Tangle Breeches, and Kinkawoodles.

Linzer Hearts

············

The world-famous torte from Linz, Austria, inspired these butter-rich hazelnut and raspberry cookies. The light pastry texture and festive lattice top make them popular at Christmas, though our 6-inch hearts are a special sweet for Valentine's Day, too.

MAKES 6 LARGE COOKIES

½ cup sugar
¾ cup (1½ sticks) butter or
    margarine, softened
1 egg
1 teaspoon vanilla extract
1 teaspoon grated lemon rind
2 cups all-purpose flour

1 cup ground hazelnuts or
    almonds
½ teaspoon salt
½ teaspoon ground
    cinnamon
⅛ teaspoon ground allspice
9 tablespoons seedless
    raspberry preserves

1. Set aside 1 tablespoon sugar. In a large bowl, with an electric mixer on medium speed, beat the butter and the remaining sugar until light and fluffy. Beat in the egg, vanilla, and lemon rind.

2. Reduce the mixer speed to low, and beat in the flour, ground hazelnuts, salt, cinnamon, and allspice, scraping the bowl occasionally, until well combined. Refrigerate the dough several hours, or until the dough is stiff enough to roll out.

3. Divide the dough into thirds. Between 2 pieces of waxed paper, roll out two thirds of the dough to a ¼-inch thickness. Freeze the rolled dough for 10 minutes to make it more manageable.

4. Grease 2 baking sheets. Remove the top piece of waxed paper from the rolled dough. With a lightly floured, 6-inch scalloped heart-shaped cookie cutter, or a 6-inch heart-shaped cardboard template and a fluted pastry wheel, cut out 6 cookie hearts from the rolled dough; reserve the scraps. Place the hearts, about 1 inch apart, on the prepared baking sheets. Spread 1½ tablespoons raspberry preserves onto each cookie.

5. On lightly floured waxed paper, roll out the remaining dough with the reserved scraps into a 12- by 9-inch rectangle. Freeze the rectangle for 10 minutes to make it more manageable.

6. Heat the oven to 375°F. With a fluted pastry wheel or sharp knife, cut the rectangle lengthwise into 18 strips; cut the strips crosswise in half to make thirty-six 6- by ½-inch strips. On each cookie heart, place 3 strips on the preserves, evenly spaced in one direction, and 3 strips in the opposite direction to form a mock lattice. Trim the extra pastry strip ends. Sprinkle some of the reserved 1 tablespoon sugar onto the lattice on each cookie.

7. Bake the cookies 16 to 18 minutes, or until firm and golden. Cool the cookies completely on wire racks.

TIPS FOR COOKIE SUCCESS

Because cookie recipes are so short and seem familiar, bakers sometimes overlook ingredients and inadvertently skip a direction, so do pay attention.

• Assemble and mix ingredients carefully.

• When baking drop, cut, pressed, or giant cookies, make sure that all portions of dough on the baking sheet are the same size. This ensures even baking.

• Space the dough evenly, and try to leave no large bare spots on the baking sheet.

• Preheat the oven for at least 10 minutes.

• Use rimless or low-rimmed baking sheets for better heat circulation during baking and for easy removal of the cookies to the cooling rack.

• A shiny, reflective aluminum baking sheet will do a better job of baking cookies to an even golden color than will a dark metal sheet.

• Place the baking sheet in the oven so that there are at least 2 inches between the pan and the oven wall.

• If baking two sheets at a time, rotate their position on the racks halfway through baking to ensure even baking and a uniform color.

• As soon as the cookies are firm enough, remove them from the hot baking sheet. Don't ever allow them to "cool" on the baking sheet because they won't cool at all — they'll actually continue to cook.

Benne Seed Wafers

Some claim that benne, an old Southern word for sesame seed, was carried here on slave ships for good luck. It is still called benne in the South, and its nutty sesame flavor is integral to much Southern cooking and a must in these crisp melt-in-your-mouth wafers.

MAKES 4½ DOZEN WAFERS

½ cup sesame seeds
1 cup all-purpose flour
¼ teaspoon baking soda
⅛ teaspoon salt
½ cup (1 stick) butter,
    softened

½ cup firmly packed
    light-brown sugar
1 egg
1 teaspoon vanilla extract

1. In a heavy skillet, heat the sesame seeds over medium heat, stirring constantly, until golden. Remove from the heat and cool to room temperature.

2. In a small bowl, combine the flour, baking soda, and salt; set aside. In a large bowl, with an electric mixer on medium speed, beat the butter, brown sugar, egg, and vanilla until smooth. Reduce the mixer speed to low, and beat in the flour mixture; stir in the sesame seeds. Cover and refrigerate the dough 2 hours, or overnight.

3. Let the dough stand at room temperature until it is soft enough to spoon out. Heat the oven to 375°F. Drop the dough by slightly rounded measuring teaspoonfuls onto ungreased baking sheets, 1½-inches apart.

4. Bake the wafers 8 to 10 minutes, or until lightly browned around the edges. Cool the wafers on the baking sheets on wire racks for 1 minute. Remove the wafers from the baking sheets and cool completely on the racks.

READY DOUGH

It's possible to have dough ready-made and on hand for an "improvised" batch of cookies. Most dough will keep up to three days, covered, in the refrigerator.

Coconut Macaroons

The classic macaroon is basically a meringue cookie that is flavored with almond paste or ground almonds. This version of a coconut macaroon is so simple that a child could easily make them.

MAKES 1½ DOZEN COOKIES

2 7-ounce packages flaked
coconut
1 14-ounce can sweetened
condensed milk,
(not evaporated milk)

2 teaspoons almond or
vanilla extract

1. Heat the oven to 350°F. Cover several baking sheets with aluminum foil; generously grease the foil.

2. In a large bowl, combine the coconut, condensed milk, and almond extract. Drop the mixture by generous teaspoonfuls, about 2 inches apart, onto the prepared baking sheets.

3. Bake the macaroons 8 to 10 minutes, or until the edges are golden brown. Remove the macaroons from the baking sheets immediately and cool completely on greased wire racks.

COOKIE CUTTERS!

If you haven't done so already, start a collection of cookie cutters. Any cookware store is a good place to begin. Nowadays there are cookie cutters to honor every hobby, occupation, or theme imaginable: bears, dinosaurs, dolphins, boats, trees, football helmets, baseballs, racing cars, hammers, airplanes, saws, exquisitely fluted flowers — even the Empire State Building!

Antique and secondhand cookie cutters work just as well as shiny brand-new ones. If you can't find the cutter you like, make your own. Draw the design on heavy cardboard and cut it out. Place it on top of the rolled dough and cut around it with a sharp knife. Lift the dough cutout with a spatula and place it on the baking sheet.

Almond Oaties

The oatmeal cookie continues to be (after chocolate chip) one of America's all-time favorite cookies. These combine the best of all worlds: oatmeal, nuts, and chocolate chips. Kids adore them.

MAKES ABOUT 6 DOZEN COOKIES

1 cup (2 sticks) butter or
   margarine
1 cup granulated sugar
1 cup firmly packed
   light-brown sugar
2 eggs
1 teaspoon vanilla extract
½ teaspoon almond extract
¾ cup all-purpose flour

½ cup whole-wheat flour
1 teaspoon salt
1 teaspoon baking soda
3 cups old-fashioned rolled
   oats
1½ cups chopped natural
   almonds, toasted
1 cup (6 ounces) semisweet
   chocolate chips

1. In a large bowl, with an electric mixer on medium speed, beat the butter, granulated sugar, and brown sugar until light and fluffy. Beat in the eggs, vanilla, and almond extract until well combined. Reduce the mixer speed to low, and gradually beat in the all-purpose flour, whole-wheat flour, salt, and baking soda until well blended. Stir in the oats, almonds, and chocolate chips. Cover and refrigerate the dough 30 minutes, or overnight.

2. Heat the oven to 350°F. Lightly grease 2 large baking sheets. Drop the dough by rounded teaspoonfuls, about 2 inches apart, onto the prepared baking sheets.

3. Bake the cookies 10 minutes, or until lightly browned. Cool the cookies completely on wire racks.

Brownies (left), page 37; Zebra Cookies (right), page 57;
and Chocolate-Chip Cookies (top & bottom), page 58

Cornmeal Cookies, page 22

Lemon Squares, page 50

Apricot-Oat Thumbprints

These delicious oatmeal-based cookies actually originated in Scotland, where folks knew that oats were good for more than horse feed. The cookies are called thumbprints because cooks made depressions in the dough with their thumbs before filling them with thick delicious jam.

MAKES ABOUT 2 DOZEN COOKIES

1 cup confectioners' sugar
¾ cup vegetable shortening
¼ cup orange juice
2 tablespoons vanilla extract
1½ cups all-purpose flour

1½ cups quick rolled oats
Pinch of salt
½ cup apricot jam or
low-sugar fruit spread

1. Heat the oven to 350°F. Grease 2 large baking sheets. In a medium-size bowl, with an electric mixer on medium speed, beat the sugar and shortening until light and fluffy. Beat in the orange juice and vanilla until well combined.

2. In a small bowl, combine the flour, oats, and salt. Reduce the mixer speed to low. Beat the flour mixture into the sugar mixture. Drop the dough by tablespoonfuls, about 1 inch apart, onto the prepared baking sheets. Using a thumb or the back of a teaspoon, lightly press down the dough in the center of each cookie. Mound about 1 teaspoon jam into each depression, keeping the jam in the center of the cookie to prevent it from spreading or melting off during baking.

3. Bake the cookies 18 to 20 minutes, or until very lightly browned. Cool the cookies completely on wire racks.

QUICK TIPS

To soften butter in the microwave, wrap it lightly in waxed paper. Microwave on high 10 seconds.

Place a 1-ounce square of semisweet chocolate in a small microwave-safe bowl. Cover with waxed paper. Microwave on medium for 1 minute. Stir, then microwave on medium for 1 more minute, or until it is melted. Stir again, until smooth.

Gingham Cookies

Ginghams are rolled cookies that are made with strips of plain dough, cinnamon dough, and chocolate dough, looking like the famous cloth. The secret to working with the dough is to keep it well chilled. If at any time the strips become too soft to work with, place them in the freezer for a few minutes before continuing.

MAKES ABOUT 4 DOZEN COOKIES

1 cup (2 sticks) butter or
    margarine, softened
1 cup sugar
1 tablespoon vanilla extract
3 eggs
3½ cups all-purpose flour
1 teaspoon baking powder

½ teaspoon salt
1½ teaspoons ground
    cinnamon
⅓ cup cocoa powder
1 to 2 tablespoons vegetable
    oil

1. In a large bowl, with an electric mixer on medium speed, beat the butter, sugar, vanilla, 2 eggs, and 1 egg yolk until light and fluffy. Reserve 1 egg white in a cup; cover and refrigerate. Reduce the mixer speed to low, and beat in 2 cups flour, the baking powder, and salt until well combined. Stir in enough of the remaining 1½ cups flour to make a very stiff dough.

2. Remove one fourth of the dough; wrap in plastic wrap. Shape the remaining dough into a ball; divide in half. Return half to the bowl. Stir or knead in the cinnamon until well blended; wrap the cinnamon dough in plastic wrap. Place the other half of the dough in the bowl; add the cocoa and 1 tablespoon oil. Stir or knead the dough until well blended, adding more oil if the dough is crumbly. Wrap the chocolate dough in plastic wrap. Refrigerate the plain, cinnamon, and chocolate doughs until firm, 1 to 2 hours.

3. On lightly floured waxed paper, roll out the plain dough into a 12- by 3½-inch strip, about ⅜ inch thick. With a ruler and sharp knife, cut the dough strip lengthwise into nine 12- by ⅜-inch strips. Place the waxed paper with the strips on a small baking sheet; refrigerate the strips 30 minutes, or freeze the strips 15 minutes, while rolling out the other dough.

4. On lightly floured waxed paper, roll out the cinnamon dough into a 12- by 4½-inch strip, about ⅜ inch thick. Cut the dough strip lengthwise into twelve 12- by ⅜-inch strips. Refrigerate or freeze the strips on the same baking sheet as above.

5. On lightly floured waxed paper, roll out one third of the chocolate dough into a 12- by 1½-inch strip. Cut the strip lengthwise into four 12- by ⅜-inch strips. Refrigerate or freeze the strips as above.

6. On lightly floured waxed paper, roll out the remaining chocolate dough into a 12- by 8½-inch rectangle, trimming with a sharp knife to make perfectly straight edges. Place the waxed paper with the dough rectangle on a small baking sheet. Lightly brush the top with the reserved egg white. Remove the dough strips from the refrigerator or freezer. Lifting the strips from the waxed paper, arrange one plain strip along a long edge of the chocolate rectangle; very lightly brush with some egg white; place a cinnamon strip with one long side touching the first strip; brush with some egg white. Alternately arrange 2 more plain strips and 1 cinnamon strip with the sides touching, and brush between with some egg white.

7. Top the first layer of strips with 3 cinnamon strips and 2 chocolate strips, beginning with a cinnamon strip. Top the second layer with a repeat of the first layer of 3 plain and 2 cinnamon strips. Top the third layer with 3 more cinnamon and 2 more chocolate strips. Top the fourth layer with a repeat of the first layer. Refrigerate or freeze the baking sheet to firm up the dough. Brush the entire stack of strips with egg white. Carefully roll up the chocolate dough and strips lengthwise into a squared-off log, leaving the ends open. Wrap the dough with waxed paper; refrigerate until very firm, 3 hours or overnight.

8. Heat the oven to 350°F. Grease 2 large baking sheets. With a sharp knife, cut the refrigerated dough into ¼-inch-thick slices. Place the slices, 1 inch apart, on the prepared baking sheets. If tiny spaces appear between the squares of dough after slicing, or if the cookies become misshapen, let the slices soften slightly and, using a metal spatula, gently push the cookies back into a square shape.

9. Bake the cookies 8 to 10 minutes, or until golden and firm. Cool the cookies completely on wire racks.

Cornmeal Cookies

PHOTOGRAPH ON PAGE 18

Cookies made with cornmeal date back to Colonial America, where wheat was a rarity. At the time these cookies were often heavy affairs, but here the cornmeal is lightened with flour that adds sweetness as well as texture to the dough.

MAKES 8 COOKIES

*1 cup (2 sticks) butter or
   margarine, softened
½ cup sugar
1 tablespoon vanilla extract*

*1 ¼ cups all-purpose flour
¾ cup yellow cornmeal
Unsalted sunflower seeds*

1. Heat the oven to 350°F. Grease 2 baking sheets. In a large bowl, with an electric mixer on medium speed, beat the butter, sugar, and vanilla until light and fluffy. Reduce the mixer speed to low, and beat in the flour and cornmeal, scraping the bowl occasionally, until the mixture is well combined.

2. Between 2 lightly floured pieces of waxed paper, roll out the dough to a ¼-inch thickness. Remove the top piece of waxed paper. With a lightly floured 5-inch, heart-shaped cookie cutter, cut out 8 cookie hearts, rerolling the dough scraps when necessary.

3. Place the cookies, 1 inch apart, on the prepared baking sheets. Press the sunflower seeds lightly onto the edges of the cookies.

4. Bake the cookies 10 to 12 minutes, or until firm and golden. Cool the cookies completely on wire racks.

TOUGH COOKIES!

If the cookie bakes too long, or if it is left to cool on the hot baking sheet, it will be tough and probably not be a cookie you'll want to serve guests. All is not lost, however. Save those tough and stale cookies — crumbled, they make wonderful toppings for ice cream and frozen yogurt. They also make great cookie crusts for cream pies.

Snickerdoodles

For a century Americans have been having fun making versions of this cookie and saying its name. New Englanders bake it flat and Pennsylvanians add walnuts then roll it. Ours is a simple buttery ball rolled in cinnamon and sugar just before baking — perfect for the kids' first cookie project.

MAKES ABOUT 5 DOZEN COOKIES

*1 cup (2 sticks) butter or
  margarine, softened
1¼ cups plus 2 tablespoons
  sugar
2 eggs
2¾ cups all-purpose flour*

*2 teaspoons cream of tartar
1 teaspoon baking soda
¼ teaspoon salt
1 tablespoon ground
  cinnamon*

1. Heat the oven to 400°F. In a large bowl, with an electric mixer on medium speed, beat the butter and 1¼ cups sugar until light and fluffy. Beat in the eggs until blended. Reduce the mixer speed to low, and beat in 1 cup flour, the cream of tartar, baking soda, and salt. Stir in the remaining 1¾ cups flour to make a firm dough.

2. In a small bowl, combine the remaining 2 tablespoons sugar and the cinnamon; set aside. Shape the cookie dough into 1¼-inch balls and place the balls on a piece of waxed paper. Roll each ball into the cinnamon sugar until well coated. Place the cookies, 2 inches apart, on ungreased baking sheets.

3. Bake the cookies 10 to 12 minutes, or until firm and golden. Cool the cookies completely on wire racks.

A CLASSIC GIVEAWAY IDEA

To young baker wannabes, give an assortment of our American Classics cookies — a half-dozen or so of each, packaged in cellophane bags and placed inside a mixing bowl. Add a selection of cookie cutters, a wooden spoon, maybe a spatula and a potholder. Wrap it all in cellophane and include a recipe on the gift tag.

Spongeware Cookies

....

These colorfully frosted butter cookies get their name from the practice of actually applying the frosting with a sponge. Colored blue or brown, the frosting reproduces the classic pattern of the old New England ceramic cookware known as spongeware.

MAKES 2½ DOZEN COOKIES

1 cup (2 sticks) butter or
   margarine, softened
½ cup firmly packed
   light-brown sugar
   (for brown spongeware) or
   granulated sugar
   (for blue spongeware)
2⅓ cups all-purpose flour

Frosting:
½ cup confectioners' sugar
1 tablespoon butter or
   margarine, softened
½ teaspoon vanilla extract
2 to 3 teaspoons milk
4 teaspoons cocoa powder
   (for brown spongeware) or
   8 drops blue food coloring
   (for blue spongeware)

1. In a large bowl, with an electric mixer on medium speed, beat the butter and brown or granulated sugar until light and fluffy. Reduce the mixer speed to low, and gradually beat in the flour until a soft dough forms. Wrap and refrigerate the dough 30 minutes.

2. Heat the oven to 325°F. On a lightly floured surface, roll out the chilled dough to a ¼-inch thickness. With a 2½-inch round cookie cutter, cut out the cookies. Place the cookies, 1 inch apart, on ungreased baking sheets. Reroll scraps if necessary.

3. Bake the cookies 18 to 20 minutes, or until the edges are golden. Cool the cookies completely on wire racks.

4. Prepare the Frosting: In a small bowl, combine the confectioners' sugar, butter, vanilla, and milk. For the brown spongeware, sift the cocoa over the frosting and stir in, adding more milk if necessary. For the blue spongeware, stir the blue food coloring into the frosting. With a piece of sponge, a small ball of cheesecloth, or other clean cloth, lightly sponge the frosting onto the cookies. Set aside until the frosting is completely dry.

Gingersnaps

M ade from ginger and molasses, these probably originated in Germany. "Snap" derives from the German *snappen,* which informally means "something easy."

MAKES ABOUT 3 DOZEN COOKIES

½ cup (1 stick) butter or margarine, melted and cooled
½ cup firmly packed light-brown sugar
⅓ cup dark molasses
2 cups all-purpose flour
2 teaspoons baking soda

1½ teaspoons ground ginger
1 teaspoon ground cinnamon
½ teaspoon ground cloves
¼ teaspoon salt
1 egg
¼ cup granulated sugar

1. In a small bowl, combine the butter, brown sugar, and molasses.

2. Heat the oven to 350°F. Lightly grease 2 baking sheets. In a large bowl, combine the flour, baking soda, ginger, cinnamon, cloves, and salt. Stir the egg into the molasses mixture.

3. Stir the molasses mixture into the flour mixture until well mixed. If the mixture is too soft to handle, freeze for a few minutes. Divide the dough into 36 pieces and place on waxed paper. Roll each piece into a 1-inch ball. Roll the balls in the granulated sugar. Place the balls, 2 inches apart, on the prepared baking sheets. Do not flatten.

4. Bake the cookies 10 to 12 minutes, or until the tops are crinkled and just firm on top. Cool the cookies completely on wire racks.

MAKE BAKING POWDER AT HOME

If you run out of baking powder, your pantry may have the makings for more. For 1 teaspoon baking powder, combine ¼ teaspoon baking soda and ⅓ teaspoon cream of tartar. For larger quantities, sift together 2 parts cream of tartar to 1 part baking soda.

Spritz Cookies
PHOTOGRAPH ON PAGE 54

These Swedish specialties can be made into a variety of fancy shapes with a cookie press or piped into "circles-within-circles" as described below. It is tradition to decorate the cookies with colored sugar sprinkles (or dragées). Store carefully — they are fragile.

MAKES 6 LARGE COOKIES

1½ cups (3 sticks) butter or margarine, softened	4 cups all-purpose flour
	¼ teaspoon ground mace
1 cup granulated sugar	¼ teaspoon salt
2 eggs	2 tablespoons decorative red
1 tablespoon vanilla extract	sugar

1. Heat the oven to 375°F. Grease 2 baking sheets. In a large bowl, with an electric mixer on medium speed, beat the butter and granulated sugar until light and fluffy. Beat in the eggs and vanilla. Reduce the mixer speed to low, and beat in the flour, mace, and salt, scraping the bowl occasionally, until a soft dough forms.

2. Spoon the dough into a pastry bag fitted with a large star tip; pipe the dough onto a prepared baking sheet in a 6-inch circle. Continue to pipe concentric circles inside the 6-inch circle until the circle is completely filled in. Repeat the process with the remaining dough, leaving about 2 inches between the cookies. Sprinkle the decorative sugar over the cookies.

3. Bake the cookies 10 to 12 minutes, or until the edges are lightly browned. Cool the cookies completely on wire racks.

COOLING TIP:

To prevent warm cookies from sticking to the cooling racks, lightly grease the rack with vegetable oil before cooling the cookies.

Chocolate Cookie Hearts

....

If you don't have heart-shaped or madeleine molds on hand, you might want to buy them. These soft and rich chocolate "cakes" are so good, your valentine will surely be grateful.

MAKES 16 COOKIES

3 eggs
⅛ teaspoon salt
¾ cup granulated sugar
¾ cup all-purpose flour
¼ cup cocoa powder

½ cup (1 stick) butter or margarine, melted and cooled
1 teaspoon vanilla extract
Confectioners' sugar

1. Heat the oven to 375°F. Place heavy, heart-shaped molds in the oven to heat. If using madeleine pans, grease and flour the pans.

2. In a large bowl, with a heavy-duty electric mixer on medium-high speed, beat the eggs and salt until light and fluffy. Very gradually beat in the granulated sugar until the mixture is stiff, 3 to 5 minutes.

3. In a sifter, combine the flour and cocoa. Sift half the flour mixture onto the egg mixture. Add half the butter. Gently fold the flour and butter into the egg mixture just until combined.

4. Sift the remaining flour mixture onto the batter. Add the vanilla and remaining butter but do not add the milky white liquid which has separated from the butter. Gently fold until the flour is completely incorporated.

5. Carefully remove the hot molds from the oven. Generously grease the molds. Fill the molds three fourths full, and bake the cookies 10 to 12 minutes, or until the centers spring back when lightly pressed with a fingertip.

6. Cool the cookies in the molds on wire racks 1 minute. Invert the molds, unmold the cookies, and cool completely on the racks. Repeat the process with the remaining cookie batter. To serve, sprinkle the cookies with confectioners' sugar.

Delectabites

These simple walnut cookies are easy to make yet elegant enough for the tea tray. The secret is to roll the cookies in confectioners' sugar while they are still hot. The easiest way to do this is to spread the sugar evenly over the bottom of a jelly-roll pan and merely stir the hot cookies around until they are well coated.

MAKES ABOUT 2 DOZEN COOKIES

½ *cup (1 stick) butter,*
   softened
2 tablespoons granulated
   sugar

1 teaspoon vanilla extract
1 cup all-purpose flour
1 cup finely chopped walnuts
Confectioners' sugar

1. In a large bowl, with an electric mixer on medium speed, beat the butter, granulated sugar, and vanilla until light and fluffy. Reduce the mixer speed to low, and gradually beat in the flour and walnuts until a soft dough forms. Cover and refrigerate the dough about 1 hour.

2. Heat the oven to 350°F. Shape the dough into 1-inch balls. Place the balls, about 1 inch apart, on ungreased baking sheets. Bake the cookies for 15 minutes, or until firm but not brown. Gently roll the hot cookies in confectioners' sugar; cool completely on wire racks and roll the cookies in confectioners' sugar again.

MEASURE FOR MEASURE

There's a saying among carpenters that any baker should heed. "Measure twice, cut once." It keeps carpenters careful and makes them double-check before touching a saw to wood. We aren't suggesting that you measure twice, but rather that you be aware and attentive to the process. The number one mistake among bakers is incorrect measuring, according to cookie experts. Measure all dry ingredients using metal measuring cups and spoons. Dip the cup or spoon into the flour and scoop up enough so that the cup is overflowing. Level off the excess with a knife or metal spatula.

Orange Raisin Shortbread

....

This unusual recipe for a filled shortbread is redolent of orange. The dough is very soft, so be sure to roll the top layer between sheets of waxed paper. If the dough tears slightly as you remove the paper, simply press it together.

MAKES 16 COOKIES

Orange Raisin Filling:
⅓ cup thawed frozen orange-
*   juice concentrate*
2 cups dark seedless raisins
1 teaspoon grated orange
*   rind*

1 cup (2 sticks) butter,
*   softened*
¾ cup confectioners' sugar
2 cups all-purpose flour
½ teaspoon salt
1 teaspoon water

1. Prepare the Orange Raisin Filling: Reserve 1 teaspoon orange-juice concentrate. In a 2-quart saucepan, combine the raisins and the remaining orange-juice concentrate. Heat the mixture to boiling over medium-high heat; reduce the heat to low and simmer uncovered 5 minutes. Remove the mixture from the heat and stir in the orange rind; cool.

2. Heat the oven to 375°F. In a large bowl, with an electric mixer on medium speed, beat the butter and ½ cup confectioners' sugar until light and fluffy. Reduce the mixer speed to low, and gradually beat in the flour and salt until a soft dough forms.

3. Pat half the dough into the bottom of an ungreased 9-inch-square baking pan. Spread the filling over the dough in the pan. Between 2 pieces of generously floured waxed paper, roll out the remaining dough into a 9-inch square. Remove the top piece of waxed paper. Carefully invert the dough square onto the filling in the pan; remove the paper and press the dough down lightly to seal.

4. Bake the shortbread 30 to 35 minutes, or until the top is lightly browned. Immediately cut the shortbread into sixteen 2¼-inch squares. Cool the squares completely in the pan on a wire rack.

5. In a small bowl, combine the remaining ¼ cup confectioners' sugar, the water, and the reserved 1 teaspoon orange-juice concentrate. Spread the glaze over the tops of the shortbread squares.

Chocolate Wafers

What sets these wafers apart from your ordinary chocolate cookie are the sliced almonds in the cookie dough. For a nice additional touch, the dough is rolled in ground almonds as well. This recipe is so good, you will want to make a double batch and store the extra dough in the refrigerator, ready for baking more at a moment's notice.

MAKES ABOUT 4 DOZEN COOKIES

¾ cup (1½ sticks) butter,
   softened
¾ cup sugar
1 egg
1 teaspoon vanilla extract

1¼ cups all-purpose flour
⅔ cup cocoa powder
1 teaspoon baking powder
¾ cup sliced natural almonds
Ground almonds (optional)

1. In a large bowl, with an electric mixer on medium speed, beat the butter until light and fluffy. Beat in the sugar, egg, and vanilla. Reduce the mixer speed to low, and gradually beat in half the flour, the cocoa, and baking powder. Stir in the remaining flour until a stiff dough forms. Stir in the sliced almonds.

2. On lightly floured waxed paper, shape the dough into a 12-inch log. Wrap and refrigerate the dough until firm, 2 hours, or overnight.

3. Heat the oven to 375°F. Unwrap the log. If desired, roll the log in ground almonds. With a sharp knife, cut the log into ¼-inch-thick slices. Place the cookies, about 1 inch apart, on ungreased baking sheets. If the dough softens too much during slicing, refrigerate again. You may need to reshape the slices into rounds on the baking sheets.

4. Bake the cookies 10 to 12 minutes, or until the centers spring back when lightly pressed with a fingertip. Cool the cookies completely on wire racks.

Raisin-Pecan Crescents

....

These cookies are similar to *Rugelach*, the cookies traditionally served at Hanukkah. Cream cheese in the dough makes the cookies rich. Fill with any kind of jam, with poppy seed paste, or with the following classic cinnamon-nut-raisin filling.

MAKES 5 DOZEN COOKIES

½ cup (1 stick) butter or
   margarine
1 8-ounce package cream
   cheese
2 cups all-purpose flour
2 eggs
2 tablespoons water

Raisin-Pecan Filling:
1 cup finely chopped pecans
⅔ cup sugar
½ cup dark seedless raisins,
   finely chopped
1 tablespoon ground
   cinnamon

1. In a large bowl, with a pastry blender or 2 knives, cut the butter and cream cheese into the flour until the mixture resembles coarse crumbs. In a small bowl, beat the eggs and water. Stir about half the egg mixture into the flour mixture until a soft dough begins to hold together. Reserve the remaining egg mixture. Shape the dough into a mound; divide the mound into 6 balls. Wrap each ball in plastic wrap, and refrigerate until firm enough to handle, about 1 hour.

2. Grease 2 large baking sheets. Prepare the Raisin-Pecan Filling: In a small bowl, combine the pecans, sugar, raisins, and cinnamon.

3. Heat the oven to 350°F. On a lightly floured surface, roll out one ball of dough into a 9-inch round; lightly brush with some of the reserved egg mixture. Sprinkle about ⅓ cup filling in a thin layer over the round. Cut the round into 10 wedges.

4. From the curved edge, roll up each wedge to the center point. Place the wedges, point side down, about 1 inch apart, on a prepared baking sheet. Curve the ends to create a crescent shape. Repeat the process with the remaining balls of dough.

5. Lightly brush each crescent with the remaining egg mixture. Bake the crescents 20 to 25 minutes, or until golden brown. Cool the crescents completely on wire racks.

Shortbread
PHOTOGRAPH ON PAGE 53

This cookie is so butter-rich that it really should be baked with the help of a mold to prevent spreading, or rolled out as described below.

MAKES ONE 7-INCH MOLD OR 10-INCH ROUND

¾ cup (1½ sticks) unsalted
   butter, softened
¼ cup confectioners' sugar
1¼ cups all-purpose flour

¼ cup cornstarch
¼ teaspoon salt
½ teaspoon granulated sugar

1. Heat the oven to 325°F. In a large bowl, with an electric mixer on medium speed, beat the butter and confectioners' sugar until light and fluffy. Reduce the mixer speed to low, and beat in the flour, cornstarch, and salt, scraping the bowl occasionally, until well combined.

2. Shape the dough into a ball. Pat the dough into a lightly oiled 7-inch shortbread mold and unmold onto an ungreased baking sheet. Or, to make petticoat tails, roll out the dough on the ungreased baking sheet into a 10-inch round. Using a 4-inch dessert dish or saucer as a pattern, with the point of a sharp knife, score a 4-inch circle in the center of the dough. Remove the dessert dish. Score the center circle into 4 wedges and the outer circle into 12 wedges. Press the tines of a fork into the edge of the round to crimp the edge.

3. Sprinkle the granulated sugar over the shortbread dough. Bake the molded shortbread 35 to 40 minutes, the petticoat tails 18 to 20 minutes, or until the center is firm to the touch and the edges are brown. Cool the shortbread completely on the baking sheet on a wire rack. Serve the shortbread whole or broken into pieces.

MESSY MEASURING TIP: MOLASSES

Measuring sweet syrups like honey, molasses, and corn syrup can be a sticky affair. Grease a glass measuring cup first, then pour or scoop the sweet syrup into the cup just to the level line.

Hazelnut Shortbread

....

Shortbread is the Scottish national cookie that is rich and perfect for dunking. Hazelnuts make these extremely elegant and the butter makes them spread. Be sure to leave at least 1 inch between cookies on the baking sheet.

MAKES 22 COOKIES

1 cup (2 sticks) butter or
   margarine, softened
½ cup confectioners' sugar
2 cups all-purpose flour

½ cup ground hazelnuts
1 teaspoon vanilla extract
22 whole hazelnuts

1. Heat the oven to 325°F. In a medium-size bowl, with an electric mixer on medium speed, beat the butter and confectioners' sugar until light and fluffy. Reduce the mixer speed to low, and beat in the flour, ground hazelnuts, and vanilla until a soft dough forms.

2. Between 2 pieces of waxed paper, roll out half the dough to a ¼-inch thickness. Remove the top piece of waxed paper. With a 3-inch cookie cutter, cut out as many rounds as possible. Place the cookies, 1 inch apart, on an ungreased baking sheet. Press a whole hazelnut into the center of each cookie. Reroll scraps; repeat the process with the remaining cookie dough.

3. Bake the cookies 20 to 25 minutes, or until golden brown. Cool the cookies completely on a wire rack.

TEA COOKIE GIFT PACK

Make a gift of an assortment of tea cookies for a special thank-you or birthday present. Line a basket with two layers of cellophane that extend beyond the rim of the basket. Arrange a selection of tea cookies in half of the basket and wrap loosely with the top layer of cellophane. Fill the other half with tins of fine tea and two to four linen napkins; include a 2-cup pottery teapot if you wish. Wrap the entire basket in the bottom cellophane. Tie with a festive ribbon.

Pistachio Biscotti

....

Italian biscotti are "twice-baked biscuits" (cookies) that are made by first baking the dough in shallow loaf form and then cutting the loaf into slices and baking the slices until they are golden on all sides. The resulting cookies are wonderfully crunchy and perfect for dipping into tea or coffee or, as the Italians do, into wine.

MAKES ABOUT 40 BISCOTTI

1½ cups all-purpose flour
½ teaspoon baking powder
⅓ cup shelled unsalted
  pistachios, coarsely
  chopped

4 egg whites
1 egg
¾ cup sugar
1 teaspoon vanilla extract

1. Heat the oven to 350°F. Lightly grease 2 baking sheets. In a small bowl, combine the flour, baking powder, and pistachios.

2. In a large bowl, with an electric mixer on high speed, beat the egg whites and egg until frothy. Gradually beat in the sugar and vanilla until very thick and lemon colored, about 5 minutes. Fold the flour mixture into the egg mixture just until well combined.

3. Spoon half the batter into a 12- by 4-inch strip on one prepared baking sheet; repeat with the remaining batter on the other baking sheet. (The batter will spread slightly.)

4. Bake the strips 15 to 20 minutes, or until light golden brown. Cool the strips on the baking sheets on wire racks for 10 minutes. Remove the strips from the baking sheets and cut crosswise into ½-inch-thick slices. On the same baking sheets, place a single layer of biscotti, cut side down. Bake 10 to 15 minutes longer, turning the slices midway through baking, until light golden brown on both sides. Cool the biscotti completely on the baking sheets on wire racks.

Triple Chocolate-Chip Cookies, page 77

Almond Cookies, page 64

Sesame Cookies, page 70

Peanut Butter Cookies, page 56

Brownies

PHOTOGRAPH ON PAGE 17

According to Maida Heatter, eminent authority on American desserts, brownies were invented by a former librarian in Maine who simply forgot to add baking powder to her chocolate cake. When it didn't rise, she cut the flattened cake into squares and served them anyway. Lucky for us!

MAKES 9 LARGE OR 16 SMALL BROWNIES

⅓ cup vegetable oil
¾ cup sugar
2 eggs
2 teaspoons vanilla extract
½ cup all-purpose flour

⅓ cup cocoa powder
½ teaspoon baking powder
¼ teaspoon salt
½ cup coarsely chopped walnuts

1. Heat the oven to 350°F. Grease and flour an 8-inch square baking pan. In a medium-size bowl, beat the oil, sugar, eggs, and vanilla until well combined. Stir in the flour, cocoa, baking powder, and salt. Stir until well combined.

2. Set aside 2 tablespoons walnuts and stir the remaining 6 tablespoons walnuts into the batter. Spread the batter into the prepared pan. Sprinkle the top of the batter with the reserved 2 tablespoons walnuts.

3. Bake the brownies 25 to 30 minutes, or until the center springs back when lightly pressed with a fingertip. Cool the brownies completely in the pan on a wire rack. Cut the brownies into 9 large or 16 small squares.

HONEY

Honey is a more potent sweetener than granulated sugar and it adds moisture to the cookie dough. If you want to substitute honey for sugar in a cookie recipe, use 1 cup honey to 1¼ cups sugar. Add a tiny pinch of baking soda and reduce the amount of liquid in the recipe by ¼ cup.

Blondies

Blondies are the basic brownie without its chocolate. The brown sugar in the dough gives the cookies a caramel flavor. For a variation on the theme, stir in ½ cup chocolate chips.

MAKES 16 SQUARES

½ cup (1 stick) butter or
   margarine, softened
1 cup firmly packed
   light-brown sugar
1 tablespoon vanilla extract
2 eggs

1 cup all-purpose flour
1 teaspoon baking powder
¼ teaspoon salt
1 cup chopped walnuts or
   pecans

1. Heat the oven to 350°F. Grease a 9-inch square baking pan. In a large bowl, with an electric mixer on medium speed, beat the butter and brown sugar until light and fluffy. Beat in the vanilla and eggs just until well combined. Reduce the mixer speed to low, and beat in the flour, baking powder, and salt just until well combined.

2. Set aside 2 tablespoons walnuts and stir the remaining walnuts into the batter. Spread the batter into the prepared pan. Sprinkle the batter with the reserved 2 tablespoons walnuts.

3. Bake the blondies 30 to 35 minutes, or until the center springs back when lightly pressed with a fingertip. Cool the blondies completely in the pan on a wire rack. Cut the blondies into 16 squares.

A LIGHT TOASTING

Bring forth the flavor of almost any nut with a little light toasting in a moderate oven. Scatter the nuts on a baking sheet and place in a preheated 300°F oven. Shake the baking sheet or turn the nuts with a spatula every few minutes to prevent scorching. The whole process takes about 10 minutes. Don't overtoast; if the nuts become too dark, they will be tough and lose flavor.

Rhubarb Oatmeal Bars

Rhubarb gives these oatmeal bars their zing. Out in the mountainous West, where the rhubarb flourishes in the high altitude, this is a popular recipe.

MAKES 2 DOZEN BARS

Rhubarb Sauce:
½ pound rhubarb
without tops, rinsed, cut
into 1-inch pieces
½ cup sugar
¼ teaspoon ground
cinnamon
¼ cup water
2 tablespoons cornstarch

Crumb Layer:
1½ cups all-purpose flour
1½ cups old-fashioned rolled
oats
1 cup firmly packed
light-brown sugar
½ teaspoon ground
cinnamon
¼ teaspoon salt
¾ cup (1½ sticks) butter or
margarine
¼ cup chopped walnuts

1. Prepare the Rhubarb Sauce: In a 2-quart saucepan, combine the rhubarb, sugar, and cinnamon. Cover and heat to boiling over medium heat. In a small bowl, combine the water and cornstarch; gradually stir the cornstarch mixture into the rhubarb mixture. Return to boiling and cook, stirring constantly, until the mixture is thick and saucy, 4 minutes. Remove from the heat. Transfer the sauce to a bowl and cool to room temperature.

2. Heat the oven to 375°F. Lightly grease a 13- by 9-inch baking pan. Prepare the Crumb Layer: In a medium-size bowl, combine the flour, oats, brown sugar, cinnamon, and salt. With a pastry blender or 2 knives, cut the butter into the flour mixture until the mixture resembles coarse crumbs. Press half the crumb mixture into the bottom of the prepared pan. Spread the rhubarb sauce over the crumb layer. Top with the remaining crumbs and the walnuts.

3. Bake the batter 25 minutes or until the top is golden brown and the rhubarb mixture is bubbly. Cool completely in the pan on a wire rack. Cut into twenty-four 2¼- by 2-inch bars.

Caramel-Pistachio Brownies

Pistachio nuts add a haunting, rich flavor to this already dense and fudgy caramel-glazed dessert. For this fancy version, bake some of the batter in madeleine molds, and crown each brownie with a glazed, shell-shaped baby brownie. Bake all the batter in the square pan for a simple home treat.

MAKES 4 SERVINGS

Brownie:
12 1-ounce squares semisweet chocolate
¾ cup (1½ sticks) butter or margarine
4 eggs
1 cup sugar
1 cup all-purpose flour
½ teaspoon baking powder
¼ teaspoon ground cinnamon

Caramel:
¾ cup water
¾ cup sugar

½ teaspoon lemon juice
⅓ cup heavy cream
3 tablespoons butter or margarine, cut into pieces
2 tablespoons chopped shelled pistachios

Chocolate Glaze:
2 tablespoons heavy cream
2 1-ounce squares semisweet chocolate, ground
2 teaspoons butter or margarine

½ cup whipped cream

1. Prepare the Brownie: Heat the oven to 350°F. Grease an 8-inch square baking pan. If chocolate-glazed brownie shells are desired, grease and flour four 2-inch molds of a scalloped shell-shaped madeleine pan.

2. In the top of a double boiler over simmering water, melt the chocolate and butter. Meanwhile, in a large bowl, with an electric mixer on medium speed, beat the eggs and sugar until smooth. Gradually beat in the melted chocolate mixture. Reduce the mixer speed to low, and beat in the flour, baking powder, and cinnamon just until combined.

3. Fill the shell molds two thirds full with the batter. Spoon the remaining batter into the prepared pan. Bake the brownie shells 6 to 7 minutes, and the brownies in the square pan 35 to 40 minutes, or until the top begins to crack. Cool the brownies completely in the pans on wire racks. Remove the brownie shells from the pan.

4. Prepare the Caramel: In a 1-quart saucepan, heat the water, sugar, and lemon juice to boiling. Cook over medium heat until the mixture becomes golden brown, about 10 minutes. Carefully stir in the cream, and cook 2 minutes longer, until the mixture thickens. Remove from the heat, and stir in the butter until well blended. Pour the caramel over the brownies in the square pan, tilting the pan to make an even layer. Sprinkle the pistachios over the caramel.

5. Prepare the Chocolate Glaze: In a small saucepan, heat the cream to boiling. Remove from the heat. Stir the chocolate into the cream until the chocolate melts. Stir in the butter until well combined. Coat the brownie shells with the chocolate glaze, or drizzle the glaze over the caramel-covered brownies.

6. To serve, cut the caramel-covered brownies into 4 pieces; place each piece on a dessert plate. Spoon some whipped cream onto the center of each piece and top with a chocolate-glazed brownie shell. Serve immediately.

KEEPING IT FRESH

Keep walnuts, pecans, hazelnuts, and almonds on hand for improvised cookie batches. If frozen, nuts will keep up to a year when tightly wrapped in heavy-duty plastic bags or containers. When grinding nuts that have been frozen, be sure to let them come to room temperature before processing them in the food processor or blender.

A light toasting beforehand will enhance the flavor of the nuts and the flavor of the cookie.

Peanut Butter Brownies

Peanut butter and chocolate are the perfect match, particularly when paired in a rich, creamy brownie batter. Pay special heed to pan sizes as called for in Step 1 or you might end up with a mess in the oven.

MAKES 2½ DOZEN BROWNIES

2 cups sugar
1 cup all-purpose flour
½ cup cocoa powder
1 teaspoon baking powder
1 cup (2 sticks) butter or
* margarine, softened*

½ cup creamy or chunky
* peanut butter*
4 eggs, lightly beaten
¼ cup milk

1. Heat the oven to 350°F. Grease a 17- by 11-inch jelly-roll pan, or both a 15½- by 10½-inch jelly-roll pan and a 9- by 5-inch loaf pan. (It is important that the pan or combination of pans be large enough so that the brownies do not run over the edge during baking.)

2. In a large bowl, combine the sugar, flour, cocoa, and baking powder. In a large bowl, with an electric mixer on high speed, beat the butter and peanut butter until light and fluffy. Gradually beat the eggs and milk into the peanut butter mixture.

3. Stir the peanut butter mixture into the flour mixture until smooth and well combined. Spread the mixture evenly in the prepared pan. (If using 2 pans, place 1 cup batter in the loaf pan.)

4. Bake the brownies 20 to 25 minutes for the jelly-roll pans, 18 to 20 minutes for the loaf pan, or until a cake tester inserted in the center comes out clean. Cool the brownies completely in the pan on a wire rack before cutting. Cut into thirty 2½- by 2-inch bars.

COOL EGG

Egg whites can be frozen in a plastic container with a tight-fitting lid or frozen one egg white to an ice cube mold. Once frozen, unmold the individual cubes and wrap them well in plastic. Thaw to room temperature before using.

Prune-Nut Bars

These old-fashioned bars are loaded with goodness. Moist and dense, they will last, covered, for several days. As the perfect snack food, they are great for the lunch box or picnic basket.

MAKES 2 DOZEN BARS

1 cup plus 2 tablespoons
   old-fashioned rolled oats
1½ cups whole-wheat flour
⅔ cup firmly packed
   light-brown sugar
⅔ cup butter or margarine,
   softened
1 teaspoon vanilla extract
½ teaspoon salt

½ teaspoon baking soda
1 8-ounce container vanilla
   yogurt
1 teaspoon grated orange
   rind
2 cups diced pitted prunes
   (about 12 ounces)
1 cup chopped walnuts

1. Heat the oven to 350°F. Line the bottom and the 2 long sides of a 13- by 9-inch baking pan with heavy-duty aluminum foil.

2. In a food processor fitted with the chopping blade, process 1 cup oats until ground into a fine powder. Add the whole-wheat flour, brown sugar, butter, vanilla, salt, and baking soda; process just until combined. Add the yogurt and orange rind; mix well. Transfer the mixture to a large bowl. (Or, in a blender, grind the oats, and combine the oats and remaining ingredients in a large bowl of an electric mixer on medium speed.)

3. Stir the prunes and walnuts into the oat mixture. Spread the batter evenly in the prepared pan. Sprinkle the top with the remaining 2 tablespoons oats and lightly press into the batter.

4. Bake the batter 30 to 35 minutes, or until the center springs back when lightly pressed with a fingertip. Cool completely in the pan on a wire rack. Using the foil, lift the baked dough from the pan; invert it onto a cutting board. Remove the foil. Cut the baked dough lengthwise into 3 strips and cut each strip into 8 bars.

Coffee Snack Bars

Y ou can make these at the last minute, perhaps on the occasion of the
arrival of unexpected visitors. All the ingredients are usually handy in
the pantry. Substitute walnuts for pecans and chopped dates for raisins if
you wish.

MAKES 1 DOZEN BARS

¾ cup all-purpose flour
¾ teaspoon baking powder
¼ teaspoon salt
¼ cup instant coffee
   granules
2 tablespoons water
½ cup (1 stick) butter or
   margarine, melted

½ cup firmly packed
   light-brown sugar
2 eggs
1½ teaspoons vanilla extract
1 cup chopped pecans
½ cup dark seedless raisins

1. Heat the oven to 350°F. Grease and flour an 8-inch square baking
pan. In a medium-size bowl, combine the flour, baking powder, and salt.

2. In a large bowl, stir the instant coffee into the water. Gradually add
the butter, brown sugar, eggs, and vanilla. Stir until well combined, then
stir the flour mixture into the butter mixture just until well combined.
Stir in the pecans and raisins. Spread the batter into the prepared pan.

3. Bake the batter 20 to 25 minutes, or until the center springs back
when lightly pressed with a fingertip. Cool completely in the pan on a
wire rack. Cut into twelve 2⅔- by 2-inch bars.

COOKIES AND KIDS

O ne of the easiest and old-fashioned ways for an inexperienced
cook to separate an egg is to break the egg, allow the yolk to rest
in the web of the fingers and let the white seep through the fingers to
the bowl below — washing hands well afterwards. Kids love separating
eggs this way while they look forward to one day having the coordina-
tion to separate eggs from shell to shell. Being successful with this tech-
nique boosts confidence in the young baker.

Fig Bars

Figs were brought to America by the Spanish missionaries and are symbols of peace and prosperity. These fig bars are like homemade Fig Newtons.

MAKES 15 BARS

¼ cup sugar
⅓ cup hot water
¾ cup (1½ sticks) butter or
   margarine
2 cups whole-wheat or all-
   purpose flour

Fig Filling:
1 8-ounce package dried figs
¼ cup dark seedless raisins
¼ cup chopped walnuts
¼ cup honey
1 teaspoon lemon juice
1 teaspoon grated lemon rind
¼ teaspoon ground
   cinnamon

1. In a small bowl, stir the sugar into the hot water. In a medium-size bowl, with a pastry blender or 2 knives, cut the butter into the flour until the mixture resembles coarse crumbs. Stir the sugar water into the flour mixture to form a soft dough. Knead the dough in the bowl until it is smooth. Wrap and refrigerate the dough at least 1 hour.

2. Prepare the Fig Filling: In a food processor fitted with the chopping blade, combine the figs, raisins, and walnuts; process until finely chopped. Or, use a food grinder or finely chop the fruit mixture with a knife. Stir the honey, lemon juice, lemon rind, and cinnamon into the fruit mixture. Set the mixture aside.

3. Heat the oven to 350°F. Grease a baking sheet. Divide the dough into thirds. On lightly floured waxed paper, roll out one third into a 10-by 5-inch rectangle. Using one third of the fruit filling, spoon a 2-inch strip of fruit filling lengthwise down the center of the rectangle.

4. Lift the sides of the dough over the filling and overlap slightly. Press the flaps of dough together. Place the strip on the prepared sheet; turn the ends under. Repeat the process to make 2 more strips and place the strips on the baking sheet.

5. Bake the strips 20 to 25 minutes, or until firm and golden. Cool the strips completely on wire racks, and cut into 2-inch bars.

Fruitcake Patchwork Squares

....

Arich fruit and brandy batter, made lighter by egg whites, is the base
of this patchwork quilt design. Made of apricot and raspberry fruit
rolls, the design is up to you: Create an original or follow a
traditional quilt motif.

MAKES 2 DOZEN SQUARES

1 cup dried currants
1 cup diced mixed candied
* fruit (chop the fruit pieces*
* if larger than ¼ inch)*
¼ cup brandy, dry sherry, or
* orange juice*
5 eggs, separated, at room
* temperature*
⅔ cup sugar
1 cup (2 sticks) butter or
* margarine, softened*

¼ cup milk
2 cups all-purpose flour
½ teaspoon ground nutmeg
½ 4-ounce package apricot
* or orange chewy fruit rolls*
* (4 rolls)*
½ 4-ounce package
* raspberry or cherry chewy*
* fruit rolls (4 rolls)*

1. In a medium-size bowl, combine the currants, candied fruit, and
brandy. Cover the mixture and let stand at room temperature, stirring
occasionally, until the liquid is absorbed by the fruit, at least 3 hours.

2. Heat the oven to 350°F. Lightly grease a 15½- by 10½-inch jelly-
roll pan. In a large bowl, with an electric mixer on high speed, beat the
egg whites until foamy. Gradually add ⅓ cup sugar, beating constantly,
until stiff peaks form.

3. In another large bowl, with the same beaters and the mixer on
medium speed, beat the butter and remaining ⅓ cup sugar until light
and fluffy. Gradually beat in the egg yolks, milk, 1 cup flour, and the
nutmeg until combined. Stir in the remaining 1 cup flour and the fruit.

4. Stir about 1 cup of the egg whites into the batter; gently fold in
the remaining egg whites. Spread the batter evenly in the prepared pan.

5. Bake the cookies 25 to 30 minutes, or until the center springs
back when lightly pressed with a fingertip. Cool the cookies completely
in the pan on a wire rack.

6. To decorate the cookies: With a sharp knife, cut the cookies into
2 ½-inch squares (4 lengthwise strips and 6 crosswise); set aside. Unroll

a few apricot and raspberry fruit rolls; peel the rolls from the cellophane and place each between small pieces of waxed paper for easier handling. Using a 2-inch cookie cutter, trace a star, leaf, diamond, or any other quilt-like designs (or draw your own quilt designs) on thin cardboard and cut out to use as templates. Place the waxed paper-covered fruit rolls on a cutting board. Using an X-acto knife or single-edge razor blade, cut out the design. Peel off the waxed paper from each side of the designs and press the cut pieces of fruit roll onto each cookie square, alternating colors, if desired. Cut the remaining fruit rolls into ⅛-inch-wide strips and use to outline the cookie squares.

7. To store the cookies: With a pancake turner, place the cookies in large flat plastic or other airtight containers. Keep the cookies in a single layer because the fruit roll designs will stick to whatever is placed on top of them. Cover the containers. Refrigerate the cookies up to 1 week or freeze up to several weeks. Let the cookies return to room temperature before serving.

BAKING WITH KIDS

Cultivate a love of baking in a young child and you have given a wonderful, lifelong gift. It is important to keep expectations realistic for both you and your child, and choose a stress-free, unrushed time to bake together. To ensure early projects are fun and successful, follow these tips:

- Choose simple, one-bowl recipes.
- Assemble all ingredients beforehand.
- Let children stir, using sturdy wooden spoons.
- Have the children pick their favorite cookie cutters.
- To remove cookies from the baking sheets, have small children use spatulas with short, wide handles, that are easy to hold.
- Always make a double batch to guard against spillage, and breakage.
- Any decorations for the cookies should be easily visible in bowls, easy for children to pick through.
- If you do complicated projects such as Christmas cookies, spread the project out over two or three days.

Oatmeal Cranberry Bars

For centuries, cranberries paired with sugared oats have been a New England hallmark, but what sets these apart from other cranberry-flavored cookies is the very thick — uncompromisingly piquant — cranberry filling.

MAKES 2 DOZEN SQUARES OR 3 DOZEN BARS

1 16-ounce can whole-berry cranberry sauce	¾ cup firmly packed light-brown sugar
2 tablespoons cornstarch	½ teaspoon baking soda
1¾ cups quick rolled oats	½ teaspoon salt
¾ cup all-purpose flour	⅓ cup butter or margarine
	3 to 4 tablespoons milk

1. In a 1-quart saucepan, combine the cranberry sauce and cornstarch until well mixed; cook over medium heat, stirring constantly, until thickened and bubbly, 3 to 5 minutes. Remove from the heat. Cool the cranberry mixture 5 minutes.

2. Heat the oven to 375°F. Grease a 13- by 9-inch baking pan. In a large bowl, combine the oats, flour, brown sugar, baking soda, and salt. With a pastry blender or 2 knives, cut the butter into the flour mixture until the mixture resembles coarse crumbs. Stir in enough milk to moisten the mixture. Press half the crumb mixture into the bottom of the prepared pan. Spread the cranberry mixture over the crust in the pan. Top with the remaining crumb mixture.

3. Bake the batter 30 minutes, or until golden brown. Cool completely in the pan on a wire rack. Cut into twenty-four 2-inch squares or thirty-six 3¼- by 1-inch bars.

MIXING

Unless the recipe tells you to do so, don't beat cookie dough for a long time. Most of our recipes can be mixed lightly with a hand-held electric mixer or by hand in a bowl using a wooden spoon.

Rhubarb Raisin Squares

....

Bar cookies are the quickest and easiest cookie of all to make. They're versatile, too. These squares call for piecrust mix, which makes life even easier. You can make your own piecrust if you prefer.

MAKES 16 SQUARES

1 11-ounce package piecrust mix
1 pound rhubarb, without tops, rinsed and coarsely chopped
1 cup dark seedless raisins
1 cup sugar
1 egg
2 tablespoons cornstarch
1 tablespoon grated lemon rind

1. Heat the oven to 375°F. Grease a 9-inch square baking pan. Prepare the piecrust according to the package directions. Divide the pastry in half. On lightly floured waxed paper, roll out half the pastry into a 9-inch square. Fit the pastry into the prepared pan.

2. In a medium-size bowl, combine the rhubarb, raisins, sugar, egg, cornstarch, and lemon rind. Spoon the rhubarb mixture into the pastry-lined pan.

3. Roll out the remaining pastry into a 9-inch square. Place the square on the rhubarb filling. With a sharp knife, score the pastry into 16 squares. Cut a small slit in the center of each square.

4. Bake the squares 55 minutes, or until the pastry is golden brown and the filling bubbles. Cool the squares completely in the pan on a wire rack. Cut along the score lines into 2¼-inch squares.

A GIFT IDEA: A BOX OF BARS

Gift boxes, decorative tins, even shoe boxes lined with colored tissue paper are fine for giving brownies, blondies, and bar cookies.

Lemon Squares

PHOTOGRAPH ON PAGE 18

Fancy, very sweet, and lemony dessert bars, these can be decorated with a piped lattice frosting to make them even fancier. Store in the refrigerator, but allow them to sit at least 30 minutes at room temperature before serving, to perk up the flavor and improve the texture.

MAKES 4 LARGE SQUARES

Shortbread Crust:
½ cup (1 stick) butter or
  margarine, softened
½ cup firmly packed
  light-brown sugar
1½ cups all-purpose flour
1 teaspoon grated lemon rind

Lemon Filling:
1½ cups granulated sugar
½ cup lemon juice
½ cup water
2 tablespoons cornstarch

2 eggs
2 teaspoons grated lemon
  rind

White Frosting:
6 tablespoons confectioners'
  sugar
¼ cup vegetable shortening
1 to 2 tablespoons milk
¼ teaspoon vanilla extract

Grated lemon rind (optional)

1. Heat the oven to 350°F. Grease a 9-inch square baking pan. Prepare the Shortbread Crust: In a large bowl, with an electric mixer on medium speed, beat the butter and brown sugar until light and fluffy. Reduce the mixer speed to low, and beat in the flour and lemon rind until well combined; pat the mixture evenly into the prepared pan. Bake the crust 15 minutes, or until golden. Cool the crust in the pan on a wire rack.

2. Meanwhile, prepare the Lemon Filling: In a 2-quart saucepan, mix 1 cup granulated sugar, the lemon juice, water, and cornstarch until well combined. Heat the mixture to boiling over medium-high heat, stirring constantly; cook 1 to 2 minutes longer or until the mixture thickens. Remove from the heat.

3. In a medium-size bowl, with a wire whisk, beat the remaining ½ cup granulated sugar, eggs and the lemon rind until thick and lemon colored. Slowly beat the lemon mixture into the egg mixture until well combined. Pour the filling into the prepared crust.

4. Bake the cookies 15 to 20 minutes, or until the filling is firm. Cool the cookies completely in the pan on a wire rack.

5. Prepare the White Frosting: In a small bowl, combine the confectioners' sugar, shortening, 1 tablespoon milk, and the vanilla until smooth. If the frosting is very stiff, gradually add more milk.

6. Cut the cookies into four 4½-inch squares. Place the squares on a serving plate. Spoon the frosting into a pastry bag fitted with a small round writing tip. Pipe the frosting decoratively onto the tops of the squares. If desired, sprinkle the tops of the bars with grated lemon rind.

HOMEMADE PRIORITY MAIL

Anyone who has lived abroad, gone off to freshman year at college, spent a summer at camp, or left home for the first time knows how much a delivery of homemade cookies can touch the heart and the taste buds. Most sturdy cookies, such as chocolate chip, brownie, oatmeal raisin, and fruit bars, travel very well. Delicate crispy wafers and shortbreads if packed carefully can also arrive unbroken. Here is a packing method that once delivered two-dozen chocolate chip cookies, whole and unbroken from Southern California to a student in Berlin.

Choose a box of heavy cardboard. It should be large enough to allow at least 2 to 3 inches of packing material to surround the cookies. Line the bottom with bubble wrap, crumpled waxed paper, styrofoam popcorn, colored tissue paper, tinsel, mounds of confetti, or any other material that will provide an airy cushion between the cookies and the box. Be sure the cookies are completely cooled to room temperature before packing. Layer the cookies in the box with waxed paper between layers, leaving enough space around the edges of the layers for the packing material. Add packing material to surround. Place waxed paper over the top layer of cookies and top with 2 inches of packing material.

Use overnight or 2nd-day mail if you want to guarantee fresh delivery. However, those chocolate chip cookies took 5 days to get to Berlin and were as fresh as today's baking. You be the judge — send your package in the way that makes you feel most confident.

Fruit Bars

....

These are cakelike bars packed with raisins, dates, and walnuts. Molasses and brown sugar give them a caramel color and taste.

MAKES 1½ DOZEN BARS

¼ cup (½ stick) butter or margarine, softened
⅓ cup firmly packed light-brown sugar
1 egg
½ cup light molasses
½ cup milk
2 cups all-purpose flour

1½ teaspoons baking powder
¼ teaspoon baking soda
¼ teaspoon salt
¾ cup dark seedless raisins
¾ cup coarsely chopped pitted dates
¾ cup chopped walnuts or pecans

1. Heat the oven to 350°F. Grease and flour a 13- by 9-inch baking pan. In a medium-size bowl, with an electric mixer on medium speed, beat the butter, brown sugar, egg, molasses, and milk until combined.

2. Reduce the mixer speed to low, and beat the flour, baking powder, baking soda, and salt into the butter mixture until smooth. Stir in the raisins, dates, and walnuts. Spread the mixture into the prepared pan.

3. Bake the batter 25 to 30 minutes, or until a cake tester inserted in the center comes out clean. Cool completely in a pan on a wire rack. Cut into eighteen 3- by 2-inch bars.

O V E N   C H E C K U P

If you bake often, calibrate your oven temperature every so often. Even a trusted thermostat can cause a variance in temperature of 10°F to 15°F. Make allowances for this in setting your gauge and calculating baking time.

Shortbread, page 32

Spritz Cookies, page 26

Sugar-Cookie Butterflies, page 68

Spiral Cookies

....

This is a giant, 4-inch spiraled chocolate and vanilla cookie. Like other refrigerator cookies, the dough can be made several days ahead. This makes it easy to slice and bake whenever you want to add to the cookie jar.

MAKES 6 LARGE COOKIES

1 cup (2 sticks) butter or margarine, softened
¾ cup sugar
1 egg
1 tablespoon vanilla extract
2½ cups all-purpose flour

½ teaspoon baking powder
½ teaspoon salt
2 1-ounce squares unsweetened chocolate, melted and cooled
Water

1. In a medium-size bowl, with an electric mixer on medium speed, beat the butter, sugar, egg, and vanilla until light and fluffy. Reduce the mixer speed to low and beat in the flour, baking powder, and salt to form a soft dough.

2. Divide the dough in half. Remove half the dough from the bowl and wrap with plastic wrap. Stir the chocolate into the remaining dough and wrap. Set both doughs aside at room temperature for 30 minutes.

3. Between 2 pieces of waxed paper, roll out each dough separately to make 16- by 4-inch-rectangles. Remove the top pieces of waxed paper. With water, brush the surface of the chocolate dough. Invert the plain dough onto the chocolate dough. Remove the waxed paper from the plain dough. With water, brush the surface of the dough. From the 4-inch edge, roll up the dough tightly, jelly-roll fashion. Stand the roll on one end, and gently press down to make a 4-inch-diameter roll. Wrap and refrigerate the dough at least 2 hours.

4. Heat the oven to 375°F. Grease 2 baking sheets. With a sharp knife, slice the roll crosswise into six ½-inch-thick rounds. Place the rounds, 2 inches apart, on the prepared baking sheets.

5. Bake the cookies 10 to 12 minutes, or until lightly browned and firm. Cool the cookies completely on wire racks.

Peanut Butter Cookies
PHOTOGRAPH ON PAGE 36

These can be made, like the traditional smaller peanut butter cookie, by rolling spoonfuls of dough into twenty-four ¾-inch balls and pressing each with the back of a fork before baking. Bake at 350°F for 8 to 10 minutes. For best flavor and texture, we like ordinary supermarket peanut butter, not the gourmet or health-food store variety.

MAKES 6 LARGE COOKIES

1 cup firmly packed light-brown sugar
½ cup (1 stick) butter or margarine, softened
½ cup chunky peanut butter

1 egg
2 teaspoons vanilla extract
1½ cups all-purpose flour
1 teaspoon baking powder
¼ teaspoon salt

1. Heat the oven to 375°F. Grease 2 baking sheets. In a large bowl, with an electric mixer on medium speed, beat the brown sugar, butter, and peanut butter until light and fluffy. Beat in the egg and vanilla. Reduce the mixer speed to low, and beat in the flour, baking powder, and salt, scraping the bowl occasionally, until a soft dough forms.

2. Drop the dough by ⅓ cupfuls, 3 inches apart, onto the prepared baking sheets. Shape the dough into 4-inch rounds. With a metal skewer or the top edge of a large knife, press 5 lines, evenly spaced, across the top of each cookie. Press 5 lines crossing in the opposite direction.

3. Bake the cookies 10 to 12 minutes, or until firm and golden. Cool the cookies completely on wire racks.

FRUIT BUYING TIP:

When it comes to buying dried fruit for cookies and cakes, it's good to have an idea of what you get for what you buy:

Raisins, seedless, 1 pound ----------3½ cups
Figs, dried, 1 pound --------2⅔ cups chopped
Prunes, dried with pits, 1 pound -----2½ cups
Dates, with pits, 1 pound -----------2½ cups

Zebra Cookies
PHOTOGRAPH ON PAGE 17

Named for their black and white stripes, these buttery cookies are eye-catchers in a glass cookie jar or on a dessert buffet. You will need a little patience to make them. A cookie press will help but if you don't have one, divide each color dough in half and pat into strips 3 inches wide and ¼-inch thick. Stack the strips, in alternating colors. Wrap and refrigerate overnight. When ready to bake, slice the dough and bake as directed below.

MAKES 5 DOZEN COOKIES

¾ cup (1½ sticks)butter or
   margarine, softened
½ cup sugar
2 eggs
2 teaspoons vanilla extract

2¼ cups all-purpose flour
1 1-ounce square
   unsweetened chocolate,
   melted and cooled

1. In a medium-size bowl, with an electric mixer on medium speed, beat the butter, sugar, eggs, and vanilla until well combined. Reduce the mixer speed to low, and beat in the flour until a soft dough forms.

2. Remove half the dough to a medium-size bowl. Stir the chocolate into the remaining dough. Line several baking sheets or wire racks with pieces of waxed paper. Fill a cookie press fitted with a serrated plate with the light dough. Pipe the light dough onto the waxed paper in long strips until all the dough is used. Refrigerate the dough strips for 30 minutes or freeze for 10 to 15 minutes, until firm. Repeat the piping process with the chocolate dough.

3. When the strips of dough are firm, remove from the refrigerator or freezer one color at a time.

4. Heat the oven to 350°F. Working quickly, trim the edges of the strips. Cut the strips lengthwise in half and crosswise into 3-inch pieces. For each cookie, arrange 4 pieces of dough, alternating light and chocolate, with the long sides touching, on ungreased baking sheets. Repeat the process with the remaining dough.

5. Bake the cookies 7 to 9 minutes, or until the edges just begin to brown. Cool the cookies completely on wire racks.

Chocolate-Chip Cookies
PHOTOGRAPH ON PAGE 17

Ruth Graves Wakefield served them to her guests at the Toll House Inn in Whitman, Massachusetts, in the 1930s. When the Nestlé Company printed her recipe on the package of their new chocolate chip, the cookie became an overnight American success story.

MAKES ABOUT 6 DOZEN COOKIES

1 cup (2 sticks) butter or
    margarine, softened
1¼ cups granulated sugar
1 cup firmly packed light-
    brown sugar
4 eggs
1 tablespoon vanilla extract
3 cups all-purpose flour

1½ teaspoons baking soda
½ teaspoon salt
2 12-ounce packages
    semisweet chocolate chips
2 cups coarsely chopped
    walnuts, pecans, or
    macadamia nuts

1. Heat the oven to 350°F. Lightly grease 2 baking sheets. In a large bowl, with an electric mixer on medium speed, beat the butter, granulated sugar, and brown sugar until light and fluffy. Add the eggs, 2 at a time, beating well after each addition. Stir in the vanilla.

2. With the mixer on low speed, beat in the flour, baking soda, and salt, scraping the bowl occasionally, until a soft dough forms. Stir in the chocolate chips and walnuts. Drop the dough by generous teaspoonfuls, about 2 inches apart, on the prepared baking sheets.

3. Bake the cookies 12 to 15 minutes, or until firm and golden brown. Cool the cookies completely on wire racks.

WHEN GREASE IS THE WORD

A recipe directs you to either grease the baking sheet or leave it ungreased. This is important because cookies baked on greased sheets will be thinner; they will spread out while baking. An ungreased sheet retards the spreading of cookies.

Oatmeal Raisin Cookies

PHOTOGRAPH ON PAGE 71

The good-tasting combination of oatmeal and raisins is no surprise here. Bake these giant, 4-inch-round cookies until they are brown at the edges. They will firm up as they cool on a rack. To make smaller versions, drop by spoonfuls on the baking sheet and bake at 350°F for 8 to 10 minutes.

MAKES 8 LARGE COOKIES

1 cup sugar
¾ cup vegetable or
*   light olive oil*
2 eggs
1 tablespoon vanilla extract
2½ cups old-fashioned
*   rolled oats*

1½ cups all-purpose flour
½ teaspoon salt
½ teaspoon baking soda
½ teaspoon ground
*   cinnamon*
½ cup dark seedless raisins

1. Heat the oven to 375°F. Grease 2 baking sheets. In a large bowl, with an electric mixer on medium speed, beat the sugar, oil, eggs, and vanilla until well combined. Stir in the oats, flour, salt, baking soda, and cinnamon to form a soft dough. Stir in the raisins.

2. Divide the dough into 8 pieces. Place 4 pieces on each prepared baking sheet; flatten each piece of dough into a 4-inch round, leaving 2 inches between the rounds.

3. Bake the cookies 12 to 15 minutes, or until the edges begin to brown. Cool the cookies completely on wire racks.

COOKIES FOR KEEPS

When packing cookies for storage, use an airtight container and place waxed paper between the layers of cookies. Don't pack crisp cookies with soft ones; the crisp cookies invariably become soft. Stored in its own airtight container, however, a cookie can stay crisp up to a week. To recrisp soggy cookies, place them in a 300°F oven for 5 minutes and allow to cool on a rack.

Peanut Butter and Jelly Cookies

....

Actually this cookie is a sandwich — two cookies pressed together to make a peanut butter and jelly classic. We suggest grape or strawberry jelly filling for the color and taste, but if you prefer, use your own favorite jelly.

MAKES 3½ DOZEN COOKIES

1 cup creamy peanut butter
1 cup (2 sticks) butter or
    margarine, softened
¾ cup granulated sugar
¾ cup firmly packed
    light-brown sugar
2 eggs

2¼ cups all-purpose flour
1 teaspoon baking powder
1 teaspoon baking soda
½ teaspoon vanilla extract
1 10-ounce jar grape or
    strawberry jelly

1. Heat the oven to 375°F. In a large bowl, with an electric mixer on medium speed, beat the peanut butter and butter until creamy. Reduce the mixer speed to low, and beat in the granulated sugar, brown sugar, and eggs. Beat in the flour, baking powder, baking soda, and vanilla just until combined. Increase the mixer speed to medium and beat, scraping the bowl occasionally, until a soft dough forms.

2. Shape the dough into 1-inch balls. Place the balls, 2 inches apart, on ungreased baking sheets. Dip a fork into flour and press across the top of each ball to flatten into a 2-inch round. With the tip of a spoon, a canapé cutter, or a 1¼-inch removable center of a biscuit cutter, remove the centers from half the cookies. Pat together and reroll the center cookie dough to make more cookies.

3. Bake the cookies 10 to 12 minutes, or until lightly browned. Cool the cookies on the baking sheets for 1 minute. Remove the cookies to wire racks and cool completely.

4. To make the cookie sandwhiches, spread 1 teaspoon jelly on the flat side of each whole cookie. Top with the cutout cookies and press gently.

Chocolate Chocolate-Chip Cookies

These are extra-thin and crisp dark chocolate cookies loaded with nuts and chocolate chips. Be sure to leave at least 2 inches between cookie mounds on the baking sheet, as these love to spread out in the oven.

MAKES 3 DOZEN COOKIES

¾ cup (1½ sticks) butter or
   margarine, softened
½ cup granulated sugar
½ cup firmly packed light-
   brown sugar
2 1-ounce squares semisweet
   chocolate, melted and
   cooled
1 egg

2 teaspoons vanilla extract
2 cups all-purpose flour
1 teaspoon baking soda
¼ teaspoon salt
¾ cup coarsely chopped
   walnuts, pecans, or
   macadamia nuts
1 12-ounce package
   semisweet chocolate chips

1. Heat the oven to 350° F. In a large bowl, with an electric mixer on medium speed, beat the butter, granulated sugar, brown sugar, chocolate, egg, and vanilla until light and fluffy. Reduce the mixer speed to low, and gradually beat in the flour, baking soda, and salt until a soft dough forms. Stir in the walnuts and chocolate chips.

2. Drop the dough in generous 1½-inch mounds, about 2 inches apart, onto ungreased baking sheets.

3. Bake the cookies 12 to 15 minutes, or until firm. Cool the cookies completely on wire racks.

COOKIE JAR GIFT

For a gift to your favorite kid — the one who just graduated from junior high school, or the one who just got her driver's license, or the one who just left home to start college — pack a jar full of your cookie jar favorites. Choose a glass jar that shows off the cookies or a pottery jar that will serve a useful purpose when the cookies are gone.

Black and Whites
PHOTOGRAPH ON PAGE 71

Versions of black and whites have been around for generations. Frosted with half-white vanilla frosting and half-black chocolate frosting, these are simple butter cookies. You can bake them in any shape or size, but we chose big 5-inch hearts.

MAKES ABOUT 6 COOKIES

1½ cups all-purpose flour
1 teaspoon baking powder
½ teaspoon salt
½ cup granulated sugar
¼ cup (½ stick) butter or
   margarine, softened
1 egg
1 teaspoon vanilla extract
¼ cup milk

Vanilla and Chocolate
   Frosting:
1 cup vegetable shortening
½ cup light corn syrup
½ teaspoon vanilla extract
1½ cups confectioners' sugar
4 1-ounce squares
   unsweetened chocolate,
   melted and cooled
1 tablespoon cocoa powder

1. Heat the oven to 350°F. Grease several baking sheets. In a small bowl, combine the flour, baking powder, and salt. In a large bowl, with an electric mixer on medium speed, beat the granulated sugar and butter until light and fluffy. Beat in the egg and vanilla. Fold in the flour mixture and milk just until combined.

2. Place a well-greased 5-inch heart-shaped cookie cutter onto a prepared baking sheet. Drop a level ⅓ cup cookie dough into the cutter. Spread the dough evenly to fill the cookie cutter. Carefully remove the cookie cutter from around the dough. Repeat the process with the remaining cookie dough, leaving 3 inches between the cookies.

3. Bake the cookies 10 to 12 minutes, or until firm and golden around the edges. Cool the cookies completely on wire racks.

4. Prepare the Vanilla and Chocolate Frosting: In a small bowl, with the electric mixer on medium speed, beat the shortening, corn syrup, and vanilla until smooth. Reduce the mixer speed to low, and gradually beat in the confectioners' sugar until fluffy. Remove half the vanilla frosting to a small bowl; cover and set aside. With the mixer on low speed, beat the chocolate and cocoa into the remaining white frosting until well mixed.

5. When the cookies are cool, spread some chocolate frosting onto half of a heart-shaped cookie and some vanilla frosting onto the other half. Repeat the process with the remaining cookies and frosting.

COLD STORAGE

This is how some bakers we know do all their baking for Christmas absolutely stress-free. They do it several weeks — even 3 months — before the holiday and freeze everything. Frozen cookies, thawed to room temperature, taste as fresh as the day they were baked. To freeze cookies, be sure they are thoroughly cooled. Wrap them in heavy-duty plastic bags, or layer them with waxed paper between layers in airtight plastic containers.

Before packing up delicate wafers or lace cookies for cold storage, place the baking sheet with the cookies on it in the freezer long enough to make the wafer rigid. Then, pack them in airtight containers with waxed paper between layers.

To thaw cookies, either remove them from their containers and let stand at room temperature for 30 minutes or thaw them slowly in the container for about 2 hours. To refresh or recrisp the cookies, place the thawed cookies in a 300°F oven for 5 minutes. If you discover that you've thawed out too many cookies, they can be refrozen.

Cool storage: Good baking chocolate is a delicate thing. Keep it in an airtight container or a heavy-duty plastic bag to preserve flavor and prevent it from absorbing odors. Store it in a cool to moderate temperature place, which needn't be as cold as the refrigerator but shouldn't be warmer than 75°F.

Almond Cookies

PHOTOGRAPH ON PAGE 35

These are big, 6-inch square, thin and crisp cookies infused with almond flavor and layered on top with thin almond slices. Topped with ice cream or fresh fruit compote, they make a fine dessert.

MAKES 4 LARGE COOKIES

1 cup (2 sticks) butter or margarine, softened	¼ teaspoon salt
6 tablespoons sugar	¼ teaspoon baking powder
2 eggs	1 egg white
2 teaspoons almond extract	1 teaspoon water
3 cups all-purpose flour	3 to 4 tablespoons sliced almonds

1. Heat the oven to 375°F. Lightly grease 2 baking sheets. In a large bowl, with an electric mixer on medium speed, beat the butter and 5 tablespoons sugar until light and fluffy. Beat in the eggs and almond extract. Reduce the mixer speed to low, and beat in the flour, salt, and baking powder, scraping the side of the bowl occasionally, until a soft dough forms.

2. Between 2 pieces of waxed paper, roll out the dough into a 24- by 6-inch rectangle. Freeze the rolled dough for 5 minutes to make it more manageable. With a fluted pastry wheel or sharp knife, trim around the outer edges of the rectangle; cut the rectangle into four 6-inch-square cookies. Place the cookies, 1 inch apart, on the prepared baking sheets.

3. In a small bowl, mix the egg white and water until combined. Brush some egg white mixture on the tops of the cookies. Sprinkle with the sliced almonds; gently press the almonds into the cookies. Sprinkle the remaining 1 tablespoon sugar over the tops of the cookies.

4. Bake the cookies 12 to 14 minutes, or until firm and golden on the edges. Cool the cookies completely on wire racks.

Mocha Macadamia Cookies

If you love the taste of chocolate with coffee, this will make your favorite cookie list. It's a golden, caramel-colored, coffee-flavored cookie studded with chocolate chunks and macadamia nuts. Use powdered espresso for a more pronounced coffee flavor.

MAKES 5 DOZEN COOKIES

1 cup (2 sticks) butter or
*   margarine, softened*
1 cup granulated sugar
1 cup firmly packed
*   light-brown sugar*
⅓ cup instant coffee
3 eggs
3½ cups all-purpose flour

1 teaspoon baking soda
¼ teaspoon salt
1 7-ounce jar macadamia
*   nuts*
1 8-ounce package semisweet
*   chocolate squares, cut into*
*   chunks*

1. In a large bowl, with an electric mixer on medium speed, beat the butter, granulated sugar, and brown sugar until light and fluffy. In a small bowl, combine the coffee and eggs; beat the coffee mixture into the butter mixture. With the mixer on low speed, beat in the flour, baking soda, and salt just until a soft dough forms.

2. Heat the oven to 350°F. Place the macadamia nuts in a strainer. Rinse the nuts under cold water to remove excess salt. Pat the nuts dry on paper towels. Stir the macadamia nuts and chocolate into the dough. Drop the dough by slightly rounded measuring tablespoonfuls, about 2 inches apart, onto ungreased baking sheets.

3. Bake the cookies 12 to 15 minutes, or until golden and firm in the centers. Cool the cookies completely on wire racks.

BAKING TIP

Light and delicate cookies can be baked on parchment cut to fit the size of the baking sheet. This will help to prevent them from burning on the bottom. When removed from the oven, allow them to cool for a few minutes on the baking sheet, then cool them on a rack.

Swirled Lemon Cookies

These cookies are piped into tiny muffin-pan cups to give them their very pretty shape. They have a buttery, light lemon flavor and a tender texture.

MAKES 4½ DOZEN COOKIES

1 cup (2 sticks) butter or margarine, softened
1 3-ounce package cream cheese
1 cup sugar
1 egg, beaten

1 tablespoon finely grated lemon rind
1 tablespoon lemon juice
2½ to 2¾ cups all-purpose flour
1 teaspoon baking powder
About 6 maraschino cherries

1. In a large bowl, with an electric mixer on medium speed, beat the butter and cream cheese until light and fluffy. Add the sugar gradually and beat until smooth. Beat in the egg, lemon rind, and lemon juice. Reduce the mixer speed to low and gradually beat in 2½ cups flour, the baking powder, and enough of the remaining ¼ cup flour, as necessary, to form a soft dough.

2. Pat the cherries dry with a paper towel; cut each into ¼-inch pieces.

3. Heat the oven to 375°F. Spoon a small amount of the dough into a pastry bag fitted with a large star tip. Pipe swirls of dough into 1¾-inch muffin-pan cups. Put a piece of cherry in the center of each cookie. Bake the cookies 15 minutes, or until light golden brown. Remove the cookies from the cups and cool completely on wire racks.

IN THE PANTRY

A well-stocked pantry makes it easy to bake when the cookie spirit moves you. Keep flour, baking powder, sugar, raisins, vanilla and almond extracts, chocolate, cocoa powder, brown sugar, molasses, walnuts, chocolate chips, and coconut all on hand.

Chocolate Chunk Cookies

....

This is a generous 3-inch cookie of chocolate chunks and walnuts in a vanilla sugar dough. This same recipe will make about 3 dozen smaller cookies, dropped by spoonfuls on baking sheets and baked at 350°F, for 10 to 12 minutes.

MAKES 15 LARGE COOKIES

1 cup (2 sticks) butter or margarine, softened
⅔ cup granulated sugar
½ cup firmly packed light-brown sugar
1 egg
2 teaspoons vanilla extract
2½ cups all-purpose flour
½ teaspoon baking soda
¼ teaspoon ground cinnamon
¼ teaspoon salt
1 12-ounce package chocolate chunks
1 cup walnuts, coarsely chopped

1. Heat the oven to 375°F. Grease 2 baking sheets. In a large bowl, with an electric mixer on medium speed, beat the butter, granulated sugar, and brown sugar until light and fluffy. Beat in the egg and vanilla.

2. Reduce the mixer speed to low, and beat in the flour, baking soda, cinnamon, and salt, scraping the bowl occasionally, until well combined. Stir in the chocolate chunks and walnuts. Drop the dough by level ⅓ cupfuls, about 3 inches apart, onto the prepared baking sheets. Pat the cookie dough into ½-inch-thick rounds.

3. Bake the cookies 15 to 20 minutes, or until firm and golden. Cool the cookies completely on wire racks.

BIG BATCHES

To facilitate baking many batches of cookies, ready them on prepared sheets of aluminum foil that have been cut to fit the baking sheet. When you remove one batch from the oven and place the cookies to cool on the rack, fit the aluminum foil filled with the next batch on the baking sheet, and bake.

Sugar-Cookie Butterflies

PHOTOGRAPH ON PAGE 54

Made from a versatile sour cream-sugar dough, the lovely fantasy butterflies make wonderful centerpieces or table decorations and favors to send home with dinner guests. You can make smaller butterflies (about 2 dozen or so) using a 2½-inch scalloped heart-shaped cookie cutter instead of the one we use. Cut 24 hearts instead of 12. Bake at 350°F, for 8 to 10 minutes. Frost and decorate in the same way as we do the large butterflies.

MAKES 6 LARGE COOKIES

¾ cup granulated sugar
½ cup (1 stick) butter or
    margarine, softened
¼ cup sour cream
1 egg
2 teaspoons vanilla extract
2 cups all-purpose flour
½ teaspoon salt
¼ teaspoon baking soda
¼ teaspoon baking powder

Chocolate Frosting:
¼ cup vegetable shortening
2 tablespoons light corn syrup
2 1-ounce squares
    unsweetened chocolate,
    melted and cooled
1 tablespoon cocoa powder
6 tablespoons confectioners'
    sugar

Confectioners' sugar

1. In a large bowl, with an electric mixer on medium speed, beat the granulated sugar and butter until light and fluffy. Beat in the sour cream, egg, and vanilla. Reduce the mixer speed to low, and beat in the flour, salt, baking soda, and baking powder, scraping the bowl occasionally, until well combined. Wrap and refrigerate the dough until firm enough to roll, 2 hours, or overnight.

2. Heat the oven to 375°F. Grease 2 baking sheets. Between 2 lightly floured pieces of waxed paper, roll out the dough to a ⅛-inch thickness. With a 4-inch scalloped heart-shaped cookie cutter, cut out 12 cookie hearts, rerolling the dough scraps, if necessary. Place the cookie hearts, 1 inch apart, on the prepared baking sheets. With a sharp knife, split 6 of the cookie hearts in half, pushing the halves apart slightly.

3. Bake the cookies 10 to 12 minutes, or until firm and golden. Cool the cookies completely on wire racks.

4. No more than 3 to 4 hours before serving, prepare the Chocolate Frosting: In a small bowl, combine the shortening, corn syrup, and chocolate until well mixed. Stir in the cocoa and enough of the 6 tablespoons confectioners' sugar until the frosting is of a smooth and spreadable consistency. Spread the frosting on 6 whole cookie hearts. Sprinkle the cookie heart halves with confectioners' sugar. Place 2 cookie heart halves diagonally into the frosting on the cookies to resemble butterflies.

G E T   C R A C K I N G

Cracking your own nuts is a very economical way to make sure you always have plenty on hand for baking. Here's a chart to tell you what you get for what you buy:

In the Shell	Shelled
Almonds, 3½ pounds	1 pound or 3 cups
Hazelnuts, 2¼ pounds	1 pound or 3⅓ cups
Walnuts, 5½ pounds	1 pound or 3 cups
Pecans, 2½ pounds	1 pound or 4½ cups

Sesame Cookies

PHOTOGRAPH ON PAGE 36

The secret to the popularity of these cookies is the giant (8- by 6-inch) heart shape and the passionate red ribbon of nonpareils flaming across it. If you don't have a proper-size cookie cutter, make a template of cardboard. Place it on the dough and trace around it with a sharp knife to cut out the heart.

MAKES 2 LARGE COOKIES

½ cup (1 stick) butter or margarine, softened
½ cup sugar
1 egg
2 teaspoons vanilla extract
2 cups all-purpose flour

½ teaspoon baking powder
¼ teaspoon salt
Water
Sesame seeds for decoration
Small red nonpareils for decoration

1. Heat the oven to 375°F. Lightly grease 2 baking sheets. In a large bowl, with an electric mixer on medium speed, beat the butter and sugar until light and fluffy. Beat in the egg and vanilla. Reduce the mixer speed to low, and beat in the flour, baking powder, and salt, scraping the bowl occasionally, until well combined.

2. Between 2 pieces of waxed paper, roll out the dough to a ¼-inch thickness. Freeze the rolled dough for 5 minutes to make it more manageable.

3. Remove the top piece of waxed paper from the dough. With a lightly floured, large heart-shaped cookie cutter, cut out 2 cookies; if necessary, reroll the dough scraps to make the second cookie. Place the cookies on the prepared baking sheets. Score a ribbon across the hearts, if desired. Brush the tops of the cookies lightly with water, and sprinkle with sesame seeds and red nonpareils.

4. Bake the cookies 12 to 14 minutes, or until firm and golden around the edges. Cool the cookies completely on wire racks.

Oatmeal Raisin Cookies, page 59

Black and Whites, page 62

Old-Fashioned Soda Crackers (top), page 82; Cracker Wheels (bottom), page 84

Prune-Pumpkin Cookies

D on't miss making these for a Halloween party or for Thanksgiving weekend guests. Two dark, crisp cookies, redolent of pumpkin and spice, sandwich a thick nutmeg and cream cheese filling.

MAKES ABOUT 3 DOZEN COOKIES

½ cup (1 stick) butter or
   margarine, softened
1 cup granulated sugar
2 eggs
2 teaspoons vanilla extract
1 cup canned pumpkin
2½ cups all-purpose flour
4 teaspoons baking powder
½ teaspoon ground nutmeg
¼ teaspoon salt

1½ cups coarsely chopped
   pitted prunes
½ cup chopped walnuts

Nutmeg Cream:
1 3-ounce package cream
   cheese, softened
1½ cups confectioners' sugar
1 teaspoon vanilla extract
¾ teaspoon ground nutmeg

Confectioners' sugar

1. In a large bowl, with an electric mixer on medium speed, beat the butter and granulated sugar until light and fluffy. Beat in the eggs, vanilla, and pumpkin. Reduce the mixer speed to low, and beat in 1 cup flour, the baking powder, nutmeg, and salt until combined. Gradually beat in enough of the remaining 1½ cups flour to form a soft dough. If the mixture is too stiff to beat with a mixer, use a wooden spoon.

2. Heat the oven to 375°F. Grease 2 baking sheets. Stir the prunes and walnuts into the dough. Drop the dough by tablespoonfuls, about 2 inches apart, onto the prepared baking sheets.

3. Bake the cookies 12 to 15 minutes, or until the bottoms are lightly browned. Cool the cookies completely on wire racks.

4. Prepare the Nutmeg Cream: In a small bowl, with the mixer on low speed, beat the cream cheese until fluffy. Beat in the confectioners' sugar, vanilla, and nutmeg until smooth and fluffy. Cover and refrigerate for 20 minutes.

5. To make a cookie sandwich, spread a teaspoonful of the nutmeg cream on the flat side of one cookie. Top with another cookie and press gently. Dust the cookies with confectioners' sugar before serving.

Raisin Filled Cookies

Plain sugar cookies filled with aromatic fruits and jams have been sold at church bake sales and packed into school lunch boxes for as long as anyone can remember. These are especially memorable.

MAKES 20 COOKIES

Sugar Cookie:
1 cup (2 sticks) butter or
   margarine, softened
1 cup granulated sugar
1 egg
1 tablespoon vanilla extract
3½ cups all-purpose flour
2½ teaspoons baking
   powder
¼ teaspoon salt
⅓ cup milk

Raisin Filling:
2 cups dark seedless raisins
⅓ cup granulated sugar
⅓ cup water
1 tablespoon lemon juice

*Confectioners' sugar
   (optional)*

1. Prepare the Sugar Cookie: In a large bowl, with an electric mixer on medium speed, beat the butter, granulated sugar, egg, and vanilla until light and fluffy. Reduce the mixer speed to low, and beat in the flour, baking powder, salt, and milk until smooth. Divide the dough in half; flatten each half and wrap in plastic wrap. Refrigerate 1 hour.

2. Prepare the Raisin Filling: In a 2-quart saucepan, heat the raisins, granulated sugar, and water to boiling; simmer, uncovered, until the filling is thick, 10 to 15 minutes. Stir in the lemon juice. Transfer to a bowl and cool to room temperature.

3. Heat the oven to 350°F. Lightly grease 2 baking sheets.

4. Between 2 pieces of waxed paper, roll out half the dough to a ⅛-inch thickness. Remove the top piece of waxed paper. With a 3¼-inch fluted or plain cookie cutter, cut the dough into rounds. Place the rounds, 1 inch apart, on the prepared baking sheets. If the rounds are difficult to handle, refrigerate until they become manageable.

5. Spoon a rounded teaspoonful of the raisin filling onto the center of each round. Roll out the remaining dough, and cut into rounds. With a sharp knife, cut an "X" in the center of each round, turning

back the points slightly. With water, moisten the edge of one dough round topped with raisin filling. Place the "X" cut dough round on top, pressing the edges with the floured tines of a fork to seal. Repeat the process until all the cookies are completed.

6. Bake the cookies 10 to 12 minutes, or until firm and golden brown around the edges. Cool the cookies completely on wire racks. Just before serving, sift confectioners' sugar over the cookies, if desired.

THE COOKIE BUFFET

Making cookie assortments for entertaining demands a little thought. Light buttery cookies, shortbread and tea cookies, chocolate wafers, and lightly frosted and fruit-filled sugar cookies all complement each other. Large cookies should be featured on their own platter. Heavier cookies such as chocolate chips, frosted ginger cookies, and black and whites look good together. A popular way to serve bar cookies is to stack same-size bars close together — a fruit bar next to a blondie next to a brownie and so on.

Pistachio-Mint Chocolate Cookies

Although these may look like many other American nut and chip-laden drop cookies, the mysterious flavor combination of pistachio and mint gives them an exotic identity. A taste of Morocco perhaps?

MAKES ABOUT 2 DOZEN COOKIES

1 cup (2 sticks) butter or margarine, softened
½ cup vegetable shortening
1 cup granulated sugar
¼ cup firmly packed light-brown sugar
2 eggs
2 teaspoons vanilla extract

3 cups all-purpose flour
1 teaspoon baking soda
½ teaspoon salt
1 10-ounce package mint chocolate chips
1 cup shelled unsalted pistachios, coarsely chopped

1. Heat the oven to 375°F. In a large bowl, with an electric mixer on medium speed, beat the butter, shortening, granulated sugar, brown sugar, eggs, and vanilla until well combined. Reduce the mixer speed to low, and beat in the flour, baking soda, and salt until a soft dough forms. Stir the chocolate chips and pistachios into the dough.

2. Drop the dough by ¼ cupfuls, about 3 inches apart, onto ungreased baking sheets. Bake the cookies 12 to 15 minutes, or until lightly browned. Cool the cookies on the baking sheets for 1 minute. Remove the cookies to wire racks and cool completely.

A NEIGHBORHOOD SPECIALTY GIFT

An assortment of sugar-dusted Ginger Cookies, Chocolate Chunk and Mocha Macadamia cookies, and Prune Pumpkin cookie sandwiches with nutmeg cream cheese filling make an exciting gift for the serious cookie lover. Arrange them on a special gift platter, then wrap platter and cookies in clear cellophane. Tie with a festive ribbon.

Sometimes a platter of one kind of cookie, such as a dozen Marshmallow Puffs, is a visually delightful gift. Try it.

Triple Chocolate-Chip Cookies

PHOTOGRAPH ON PAGE 35

Because these big heart-shaped cookies are so packed with semisweet, milk, and white chocolate chips, you might want to make 2½ dozen of the smaller version. Drop large spoonfuls of the dough on a prepared baking sheet. Bake at 350°F for 8 to 10 minutes. Heart shape or no heart shape, your loved ones will adore them.

MAKES 8 LARGE COOKIES

1 cup (2 sticks) butter or
* margarine, softened*
⅓ cup granulated sugar
⅓ cup firmly packed
* light-brown sugar*
1 egg
2 teaspoons vanilla extract
2 cups all-purpose flour
½ teaspoon baking soda

¼ teaspoon salt
½ cup semisweet
* chocolate chips*
½ cup milk chocolate chips
½ cup white chocolate or
* vanilla-flavored chips*
½ cup coarsely chopped
* pecans*

1. Heat the oven to 375°F. Grease 2 large baking sheets. In a large bowl, with an electric mixer on medium speed, beat the butter, granulated sugar, and brown sugar until light and fluffy. Beat in the egg and vanilla. Reduce the mixer speed to low, and beat in the flour, baking soda, and salt, scraping the bowl occasionally, until a soft dough forms. Stir in the semisweet chocolate chips, the milk chocolate chips, the white chocolate chips, and the pecans.

2. Place a well-greased 5-inch heart-shaped cookie cutter onto a prepared baking sheet. Drop a level ⅓ cup cookie dough into the cutter. Spread the dough evenly to fill the cookie cutter. Carefully remove the cookie cutter from around the dough. Repeat the process with the remaining cookie dough, leaving 2 inches between the cookies.

3. Bake the cookies 10 to 12 minutes, or until firm and golden. Cool the cookies completely on wire racks.

Marshmallow Puffs

Part cookie and part confection, you may remember this puffy, coconut coated (your choice of pink or white coconut) treat from your childhood. If it wasn't made fresh at home or by somebody in the neighborhood, it was certainly for sale in packages at the market. You will need a candy thermometer to help you make the marshmallow topping.

MAKES 2½ DOZEN COOKIES

Sugar Cookie:
½ cup (1 stick) butter or
   margarine, softened
½ cup sugar
1 egg
1 teaspoon vanilla extract
¾ cups all-purpose flour
1¼ teaspoons baking powder
⅛ teaspoon salt
2 tablespoons milk

Marshmallow Topping:
Red food coloring
1 7-ounce package flaked
   coconut
1 cup sugar
2 tablespoons light corn
   syrup
¾ cup cold water
1½ envelopes unflavored
   gelatin
3 egg whites, at room
   temperature
½ teaspoon vanilla extract

1. Prepare the Sugar Cookie: Heat the oven to 350°F. Lightly grease 2 baking sheets. In a large bowl, with an electric mixer on medium speed, beat the butter, sugar, egg, and vanilla until light and fluffy. Reduce the mixer speed to low, and beat in the flour, baking powder, salt, and milk until smooth dough forms.

2. Divide the dough into 30 pieces, and shape each piece into a ball. Place the balls, 2 inches apart, on the prepared baking sheets. Flatten each ball into a 2-inch round.

3. Bake the cookies 10 minutes, or until the centers are firm and the edges are golden. Cool the cookies completely on wire racks. Place the cookies in rows on the racks.

4. Prepare the Marshmallow Topping: In a medium-size plastic bag, combine a few drops red food coloring and half the coconut. Seal the top of the bag and shake until the coconut is pink. Place the pink coconut onto a piece of waxed paper. Place the remaining white coconut on another piece of waxed paper. Set aside.

5. In a 2-quart saucepan, combine the sugar, corn syrup, and ½ cup cold water. Heat to boiling, stirring once. Simmer the mixture until it reaches 250°F on a candy thermometer, or until a little syrup forms a soft ball when dropped into cold water, 8 to 10 minutes.

6. Meanwhile, in a glass measuring cup, soften the gelatin in the remaining ¼ cup cold water. Place the cup in a small saucepan of simmering water, and stir the gelatin mixture until clear. Set the dissolved gelatin aside in the pan of hot water.

7. When the temperature of the syrup is approaching 250°F, in a large bowl with the mixer on high speed, beat the egg whites until stiff peaks form. Slowly pour in the 250°F syrup while continuing to beat. Slowly add the gelatin mixture and the vanilla, and continue to beat until the mixture cools to room temperature and is stiff, 8 to 10 minutes.

8. Spoon as much marshmallow topping as possible into a pastry bag fitted with an éclaire tip or an adaptor with no tip. Pipe a mound of marshmallow on top of each cookie, working quickly and refilling the pastry bag as necessary.

9. Dip the tops of the cookies in the pink or white coconut immediately, before the marshmallow cools. Cool the cookies completely on wire racks.

FINISHES: GLAZES AND FROSTINGS

Cookies can look bake-shop perfect with a clear sugar glaze to give them a shiny finish and a little added sweetness. Brush on the glaze as soon as the cookies come out of the oven.

Combine 1 cup confectioners' sugar with 2 tablespoons water. Stir until smooth. Brush or spoon on warm cookies.

For a spicy, pale glaze, particularly good with spice and ginger cookies, add ¼ teaspoon cinnamon or allspice to the glaze.

Spread a butter frosting over any warm cookie. Tint the frosting with food coloring for special effects. While the frosting is soft, sprinkle with silver or gold dragées, colored sprinkles, or grated chocolate.

Cheddar Crackers

....

The ingredients for most crackers are generally right at hand, which makes them easy to make. This recipe turns out a puffy crisp cracker that is permeated with a sharp Cheddar flavor. We find that it's perfect for either fancy hors d'oeuvres or simple snacking.

MAKES 9 DOZEN CRACKERS

2 cups all-purpose flour
½ teaspoon salt
¼ teaspoon paprika
¼ teaspoon baking powder
1 cup finely shredded sharp
    Cheddar Cheese

1 egg white
½ cup water
2 tablespoons butter,
    melted and cooled

1. In a large bowl, combine the flour, salt, paprika, baking powder, and cheese. In a small bowl, beat the egg white, water, and butter.

2. Pour the egg white mixture into the flour mixture and stir until a soft dough forms. Knead the dough into a ball. Set aside, covered with a clean, damp cloth and let rest for 10 minutes.

3. Heat the oven to 375°F. Lightly grease 2 baking sheets. Divide the dough in half. On a lightly floured surface, roll out each half very thinly. With a 1½-inch cookie cutter, cut the dough into rounds. Place the rounds, ½ inch apart, on the prepared baking sheets. With a fork, pierce the center of each.

4. Bake the crackers 20 to 25 minutes, or until lightly browned. Cool the crackers completely on wire racks.

COOKIE GIFT IDEA

We know of no other homemade gift from the kitchen that receives as many pleasurable oohs and aahs when it is presented than a basket of cookies. Our country crackers also make terrific gifts with cheeses, jams, and honey.

Johnnycake Crisps

....

Johnnycake is a cornmeal pancake that dates back at least to 1700. We feel that oven baking these crisps enhances the crunchy sweet texture and flavor of the corn in a way that a plain griddle cooking never could.

MAKES 2 DOZEN CRISPS

1½ cups yellow cornmeal
½ cup all-purpose flour
½ teaspoon baking powder
½ teaspoon salt

⅔ cup ice water
2 tablespoons olive or
*   vegetable oil*

1. In a medium-size bowl, combine the cornmeal, flour, baking powder, and salt. In a small bowl, beat the ice water and oil. Stir the ice water mixture into the flour mixture, until a soft dough forms. Knead the dough in the bowl until it forms a ball. Set aside covered with a clean, damp cloth, and let rest for 10 minutes.

2. Heat the oven to 375°F. Grease 2 baking sheets. Divide the dough in half. On the prepared baking sheets, roll out each half very thinly into a 12- by 9-inch rectangle. With a sharp knife, cut the rectangle into twelve 3-inch squares. Do not separate.

3. Bake the crisps 12 to 15 minutes, or until golden brown around the edges. Cool the crisps completely on wire racks; separate the crisps into squares.

CRACKER TALK

Homemade country crackers will never have the slick, clean, and uniform appearance of wheat thins or soda crackers. It's part of their character to be different from each other.

- The secret to successful crackers is to roll the dough very thin, as thin as you can. Then, gently score the dough with the point of a sharp knife, indicating where you want the cracker to break.
- Once the crackers are in the oven, watch them closely, or they will burn before you know it. If they are browning quickly, turn each cracker over to finish baking.

Old-Fashioned Soda Crackers
PHOTOGRAPH ON PAGE 72

These are a bit heavier and certainly larger than the soda crackers you buy in a box at the store. A pastry dough is what makes these slightly more complicated to mix than our other crackers, but it guarantees a layered and crisp texture that is well worth the work. You may never buy soda crackers again!

MAKES ABOUT 2 DOZEN CRACKERS

2 cups all-purpose flour
¾ teaspoon baking soda
½ teaspoon salt

¼ (½ stick) butter or
margarine
¾ cup buttermilk

1. In a large bowl, combine the flour, baking soda, and ¼ teaspoon salt. With a pastry blender or 2 knives, cut the butter into the flour mixture until the mixture resembles fine crumbs. Stir the buttermilk into the flour mixture until a soft dough forms. Knead the dough in the bowl until it forms a ball. Set aside with a clean, damp cloth, and let rest for 10 minutes.

2. Heat the oven to 350°F. On a lightly floured surface, roll out the dough to a ⅛-inch thickness. With a floured 3-inch round cookie cutter, cut the dough into crackers. Lightly grease 2 baking sheets. Place the crackers on the prepared baking sheets. With a fork, pierce each cracker all over. Sprinkle the crackers with some of the remaining ¼ teaspoon salt. Knead the scraps together. Cut out and bake more crackers until all the dough is used.

3. Bake the crackers 15 to 20 minutes, or until lightly browned around the edges. Cool the crackers completely on wire racks.

CRACKER CHARACTER

The best thing about a cracker is that it's very simple to make. It takes few ingredients — flour, water, salt, sometimes cheese, oatmeal, whole-wheat flour, or cornmeal. The simplicity and the snappy result can make crackers as habit-forming as any cookie or confection.

Whole-Wheat Crackers

....

These have a very light wheat flavor. Cut into 1½-inch squares, these are ideal with soft cheeses. Or, pack several into school lunch boxes.

MAKES ABOUT 6 DOZEN CRACKERS

1 cup all-purpose flour
1 cup whole-wheat flour
½ teaspoon baking powder
¼ teaspoon salt

¼ cup (½ stick) butter or
  margarine
½ cup ice water

1. In a medium-size bowl, combine the all-purpose flour, whole-wheat flour, baking powder, and salt. With a pastry blender or 2 knives, cut the butter into the flour mixture until the mixture resembles fine crumbs. Stir the ice water into the flour mixture to form a soft dough. Knead the dough in the bowl until it forms a ball. Set aside, covered with a clean, damp cloth, and let rest for 10 minutes.

2. Heat the oven to 375°F. Lightly grease 2 baking sheets. Divide the dough in half. On the prepared baking sheets, roll out each half very thinly into a 9-inch square.

3. With a sharp knife, cut the square into 1½-inch square crackers. Do not separate. With a fork, pierce each cracker once diagonally.

4. Bake the crackers 12 to 15 minutes, or until lightly browned. Cool the crackers completely on wire racks. Separate the crackers.

KEEPING THE CRACKER

Crackers stay crisp when stored in tightly covered airtight containers — tins, jars with tight-fitting lids, plastic storage boxes. If the crackers get limp, revive and recrisp them in a preheated 300°F oven for 5 minutes.

Cracker Wheels
PHOTOGRAPH ON PAGE 72

These cracker wheels are quick-rising, thanks to a healthy dose of rapid-rising yeast in the dough. Each bakes in a two-step method — first on the baking sheet and second, on the top rack of the oven.

MAKES 1 DOZEN CRACKERS

5 cups all-purpose flour	1⅔ cups hot water
2 teaspoons salt	(125° F to 130° F)
1 package rapid-rising dry yeast	Sesame seeds (optional)

1. Heat the oven to 375°F. Arrange the 2 oven racks 4 inches apart in the oven. Lightly grease 2 unrimmed baking sheets.

2. In a large bowl, combine the flour, 1½ teaspoons salt, and the yeast. Stir in the hot water to form a soft dough.

3. Knead the dough in the bowl until it forms a ball. Turn the dough onto a lightly floured surface and knead until smooth, 3 minutes.

4. Divide the dough into 12 balls. Let rest, covered, with a clean, damp cloth 10 minutes. Roll out each ball into a 6-inch round. Place 2 rounds on a prepared baking sheet; sprinkle the tops with some of the remaining ½ teaspoon salt. With a fork, pierce each cracker a number of times, or, with a knife, score the top of the cracker to divide it into 6 wedges. With water, moisten the crackers slightly and sprinkle with sesame seeds, if desired.

5. Bake the crackers on the bottom rack of the oven, 5 minutes, or until they slide around when the baking sheet is gently shaken. Slide the crackers onto the top rack in the oven. Remove the baking sheet. Continue baking the crackers on the top rack 10 to 12 minutes, or until crisp and golden. Cool completely on a wire rack.

6. Continue baking the crackers, 2 at a time, starting on the bottom rack and finishing on the top until all the crackers are baked. Slide the crackers onto the top rack without the baking sheet. Remove each cracker as it is ready and cool completely on a wire rack.

Cornmeal Crisps

These are lighter crackers than our Johnnycake Crisps and the flavor of red pepper gives them a spicy Southwestern distinction. Serve these as snacks or with any number of creamy herb dips.

MAKES ABOUT 6½ DOZEN CRACKERS

1 cup all-purpose flour
1 cup yellow cornmeal
½ teaspoon baking powder
½ teaspoon salt
¼ teaspoon ground red
pepper or chili powder
(optional)

1 egg white
2 tablespoons olive or
vegetable oil
½ cup ice water

1. In a medium-size bowl, combine the flour, cornmeal, baking powder, salt, and, if desired, red pepper. In a small bowl, beat the egg white, oil, and ice water. Stir the egg white mixture into the flour mixture to form a soft dough. Knead the dough in the bowl until it forms a ball. Set aside, covered with a clean, damp cloth and let rest for 10 minutes.

2. Heat the oven to 375°F. Lightly grease 2 baking sheets. Divide the dough in half. On a prepared baking sheet, roll out each half very thinly into a 10- by 8-inch rectangle.

3. With a sharp knife, cut the rectangles into 2-inch squares. Cut each square in half diagonally to make a triangular cracker. Do not separate.

4. Bake the crackers 12 to 15 minutes, or until golden brown. Cool the crackers completely on wire racks. Separate the crackers into triangles.

Equivalents Table

EQUIVALENTS FOR COMMON INGREDIENTS

Granulated sugar ~~~~~~~~~~1 pound ~~~~~~~~~~~~~~~~~~~~~~~~~~~2 cups
Brown sugar ~~~~~~~~~~~~~1 pound ~~~~~~~~~~~~~~~~~~~~~~~~2¼ cups
Confectioners' sugar ~~~~~~~1 pound ~~~~~~~~~~~~~~~~~~~~~~~~4 cups
Cocoa powder ~~~~~~~~~~~~1 pound ~~~~~~~~~~~~~~~~~~~~~~~~~4 cups
Hazelnuts ~~~~~~~~~~~~~~~1 pound ~~~~~~~~~~~~~~~~~~~~~~~~~3⅓ cups
Walnuts, chopped ~~~~~~~~~4 ounces~~~~~~~~~~~~~~~~~~~~~~~~~~~¾ cup
Almonds, whole ~~~~~~~~~5⅓ ounces ~~~~~~~~~~~~~~~~~~~~~~~~~~1 cup
    Unblanched, slivered ~~~~1 pound ~~~~~~~~~~~~~~~~~~~~~~~3½ cups
Flour, unsifted ~~~~~~~~~~~2½ ounces~~~~~~~~~~~~~~~~~~~~~~~~~~½ cup
                3½ ounces~~~~~~~~~~~~~~~~~~~~~~~~~~¾ cup
                5 ounces ~~~~~~~~~~~~~~~~~~~~~~~~~1 cup
Cornmeal ~~~~~~~~~~~~~~~4 ounces~~~~~~~~~~~~~~~~~~~~~~~~~~¾ cup
Rolled oats ~~~~~~~~~~~~~~4 ounces ~~~~~~~~~~~~~~~~~~2⅔ cups uncooked
Lemon ~~~~~~~~~~~~~~~~~~~~~~~1 ~~~~~~~~~~~~1 to 3 tablespoons juice
                1 ~~~~~~~1 to 1½ teaspoons grated rind
Butter ~~~~~~~~~~~~~~~~~~~~½ ounce ~~~~~~~~~~~~~1 tablespoon (⅛ stick)
                2 ounces~~~~~~~~~~~~~4 tablespoons (½ stick)
                4 ounces ~~~~~~~~~~~~~8 tablespoons (1 stick)
Cream cheese ~~~~~~~~~~~~3 ounces ~~~~~~~~~~~~~~~~~~~~6 tablespoons

MEASURING EQUIVALENTS

3 teaspoons ~~~~~~~~~~~~~~~~~~~~~~~~1 tablespoon
8 tablespoons~~~~~~~~~~~~~~~~~~~~~~~~~~~~½ cup
16 tablespoons ~~~~~~~~~~~~~~~~~~~~~~~~~~1 cup
1 liquid ounce ~~~~~~~~~~~~~~~~~~~~~~2 tablespoons
4 liquid ounces ~~~~~~~~~~~~~~~~~~~~~~~~~½ cup
2 cups ~~~~~~~~~~~~~~~~~~~~~~~~~~~~~1 pint
4 cups~~~~~~~~~~~~~~~~~~~~~~~~~~~~~~1 quart
4 quarts~~~~~~~~~~~~~~~~~~~~~~~~~~~~1 gallon
1 pound ~~~~~~~~~~~~~~~~~~~~~~~~~~~16 ounces

Conversions Table

....

WEIGHTS

OUNCES & POUNDS	METRIC EQUIVALENTS
¼ ounce	7 grams
⅓ ounce	10 grams
½ ounce	14 grams
1 ounce	28 grams
1¾ ounces	50 grams
2 ounces	57 grams
2⅔ ounces	75 grams
3 ounces	85 grams
3½ ounces	100 grams
4 ounces (¼ pound)	114 grams
6 ounces	170 grams
8 ounces (½ pound)	227 grams
9 ounces	250 grams
16 ounces (1 pound)	464 grams
1.1 pounds	500 grams
2.2 pounds	1,000 grams (1 kilogram)

TEMPERATURES

°F (FAHRENHEIT)	°C (CENTIGRADE OR CELSIUS)
32 (water freezes)	0
108-110 (warm)	42-43
140	60
203 (water simmers)	95
212 (water boils)	100
225 (very slow oven)	107.2
245	120
266	130
300 (slow oven)	149
350 (moderate oven)	177
375	191
400 (hot oven)	205
425	218
450	232
500 (very hot oven)	260

LIQUID MEASURES

tsp.: teaspoon
Tbs.: tablespoon
8 ounces = 1 cup

U.S. SPOONS & CUPS	METRIC EQUIVALENTS
1 tsp.	5 milliliters
2 tsp.	10 milliliters
3 tsp. (1 Tbs.)	15 milliliters
3⅓ Tbs.	½ deciliter (50 milliliters)
¼ cup	60 milliliters
⅓ cup	85 milliliters

U.S. SPOONS & CUPS	METRIC EQUIVALENTS
⅓ cup + 1 Tbs.	1 deciliter (100 milliliters)
1 cup	240 milliliters
1 cup + 1¼ Tbs.	¼ liter
2 cups	480 milliliters
2 cups + 2½ Tbs.	½ liter
4 cups	960 milliliters
4⅓ cups	1 liter (1,000 milliliters)

Index

Almond Cookies----------------64
Almond Oaties ---------------16
Apricot-Oat Thumbprints ------19

Benne Seed Wafers ------------14
Black and Whites ------------62
Blondies -------------------38
Brownies--------------------37

Caramel-Pistachio Brownies ---40
Cheddar Crackers -----------80
Chocolate-Chip Cookies ------58
Chocolate Chocolate-Chip
  Cookies-------------------61
Chocolate Chunk Cookies -----67
Chocolate Cookie Hearts ------27
Chocolate Wafers ------------30
Coconut Macaroons-----------15
Coffee Snack Bars------------44
Cornmeal Cookies -----------22
Cornmeal Crisps-------------85
Cracker Wheels -------------84

Delectabites -----------------28

Fig Bars --------------------45
Fruit Bars ------------------52
Fruitcake Patchwork Squares ---46

Gingersnaps -----------------25
Gingham Cookies -----------20

Hazelnut Shortbread ---------33
Hermits---------------------11

Johnnycake Crisps -----------81

Lemon Squares---------------50
Linzer Hearts --------------12

Marshmallow Puffs ----------78
Mocha Macadamia Cookies ----65

Oatmeal Cranberry Bars-------48
Oatmeal Raisin Cookies-------59
Old-Fashioned Soda
  Crackers ------------------82
Orange Raisin Shortbread -----29

Peanut Butter and Jelly Cookies-60
Peanut Butter Brownies -------42
Peanut Butter Cookies --------56
Pistachio Biscotti ------------34
Pistachio-Mint Chocolate
  Cookies -------------------76
Prune-Nut Bars -------------43
Prune-Pumpkin Cookies-------73

Raisin Filled Cookies ---------74
Rhubarb Oatmeal Bars --------39
Rhubarb Raisin Squares -------49

Sesame Cookies -------------70
Snickerdoodles --------------23
Spongeware Cookies ---------24
Spiral Cookies --------------55
Spritz Cookies --------------26
Sugar-Cookie Butterflies -------68
Swirled Lemon Cookies -------66

Triple Chocolate-Chip
  Cookies -------------------77

Whole-Wheat Crackers --------83

Zebra Cookies --------------57